I0454629

MONSTER MOUSSAKA

COLORING BOOK

BY ROCK ROULADE COCOON COLLECTIVE

In a world of creatures, strange and wild,
Funny monsters bring forth a joyful smile.
They're goofy, quirky, zany, and more,
With qualities that we all adore.

They stumble and bumble, so very clumsy,
Yet their antics are nothing but pure fancy.
In their comical ways, they make us laugh,
Their playful spirit, down every path.

Mischievous monsters, misfits of glee,
Eccentric and whimsical, for all to see.
Their oddball charm, so colorful and bright,
Is a source of wonder and sheer delight.

With expressive faces, and charisma untamed,
They've captured our hearts, they can't be blamed.
Lighthearted and absurd, in a world so wacky,
These funny monsters are far from tacky.

So let's celebrate these creatures so grand,
In this whimsical, comical, enchanted land.
And when the feast is set, with laughter as our mantra,
Take a bite of Monster Moussaka!

In their charming world, where laughter is key,
Funny monsters remind us to let our hearts be free.
With every giggle, chuckle, and hoot,
They bring joy to our lives, in every pursuit.

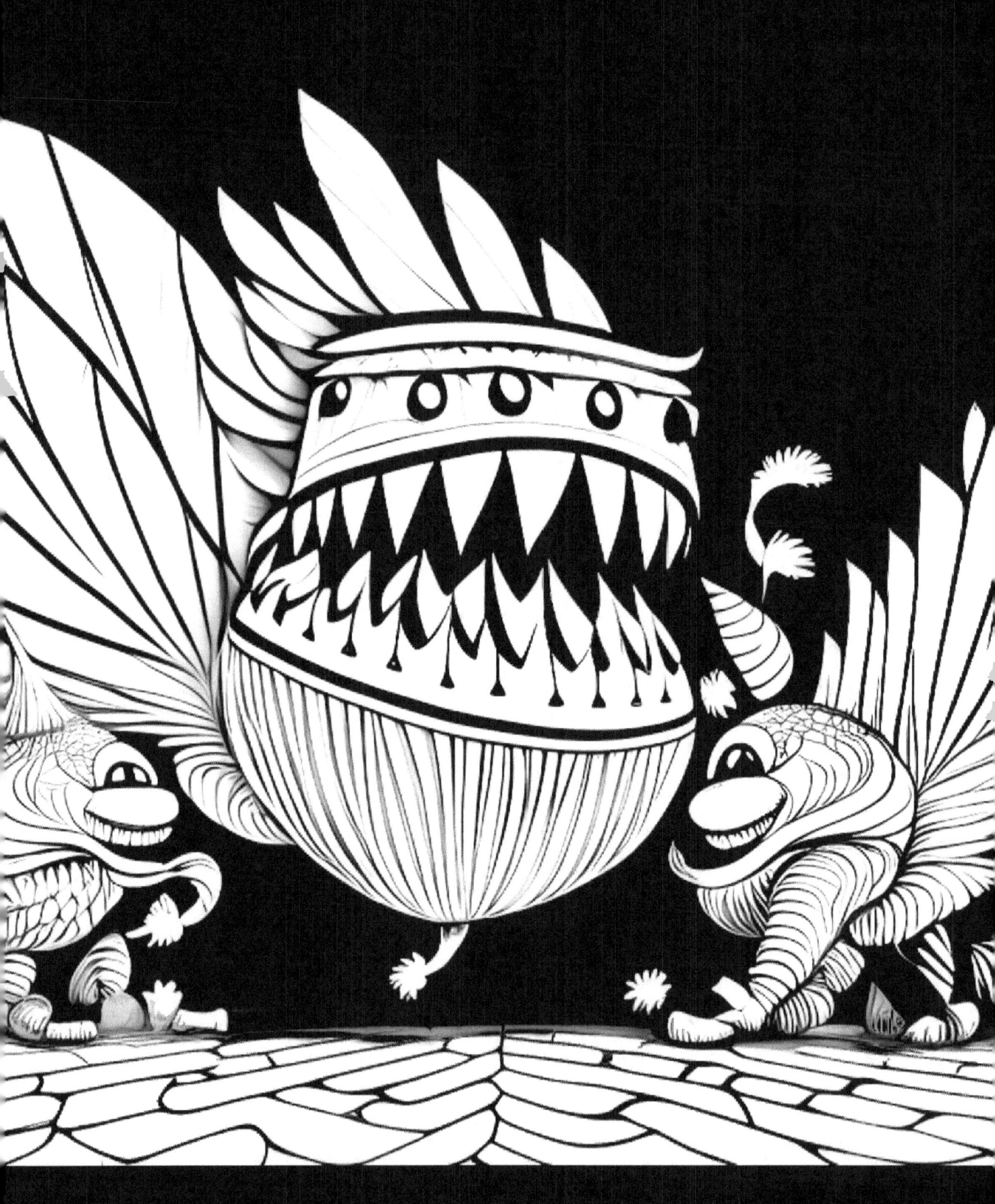

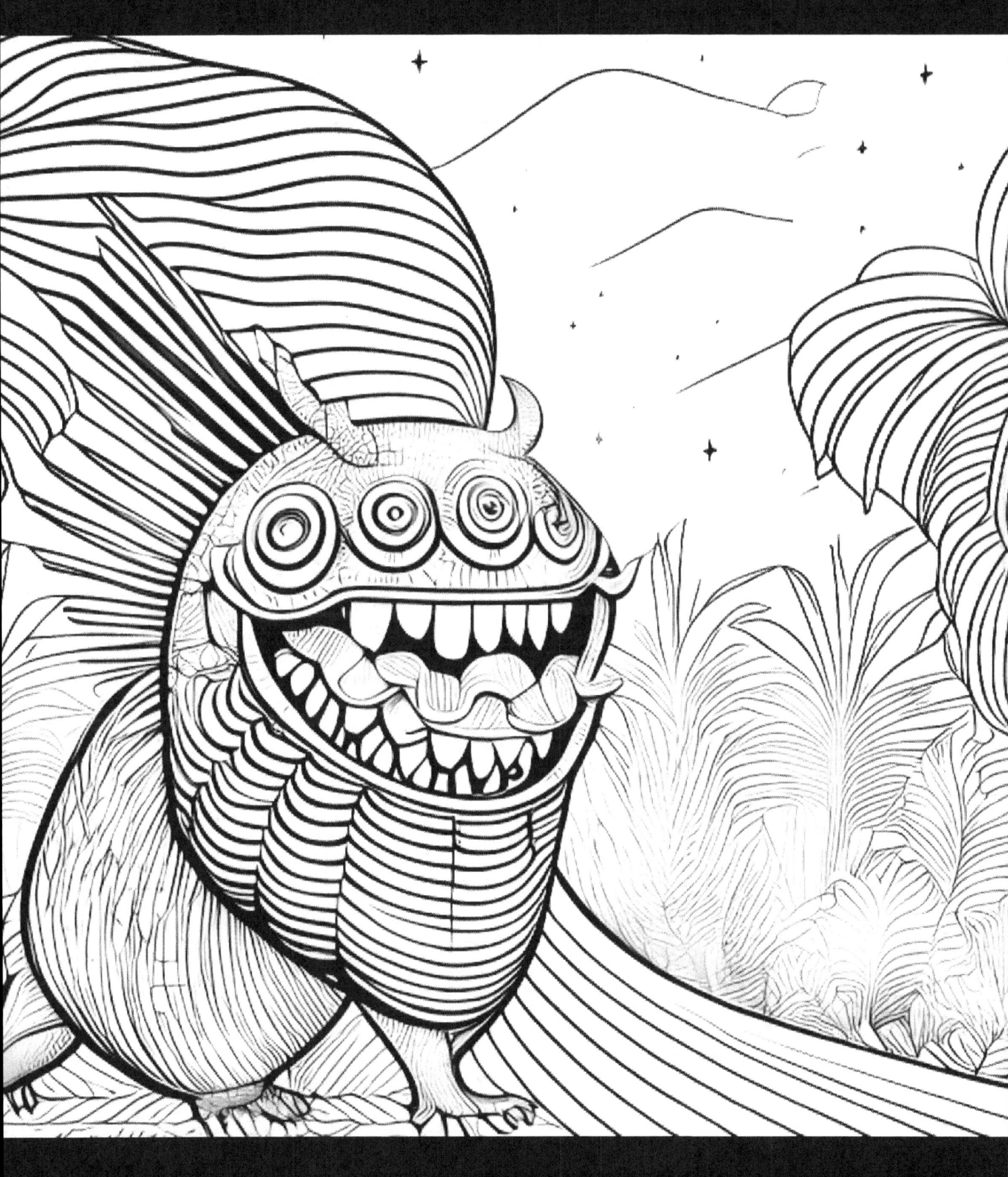

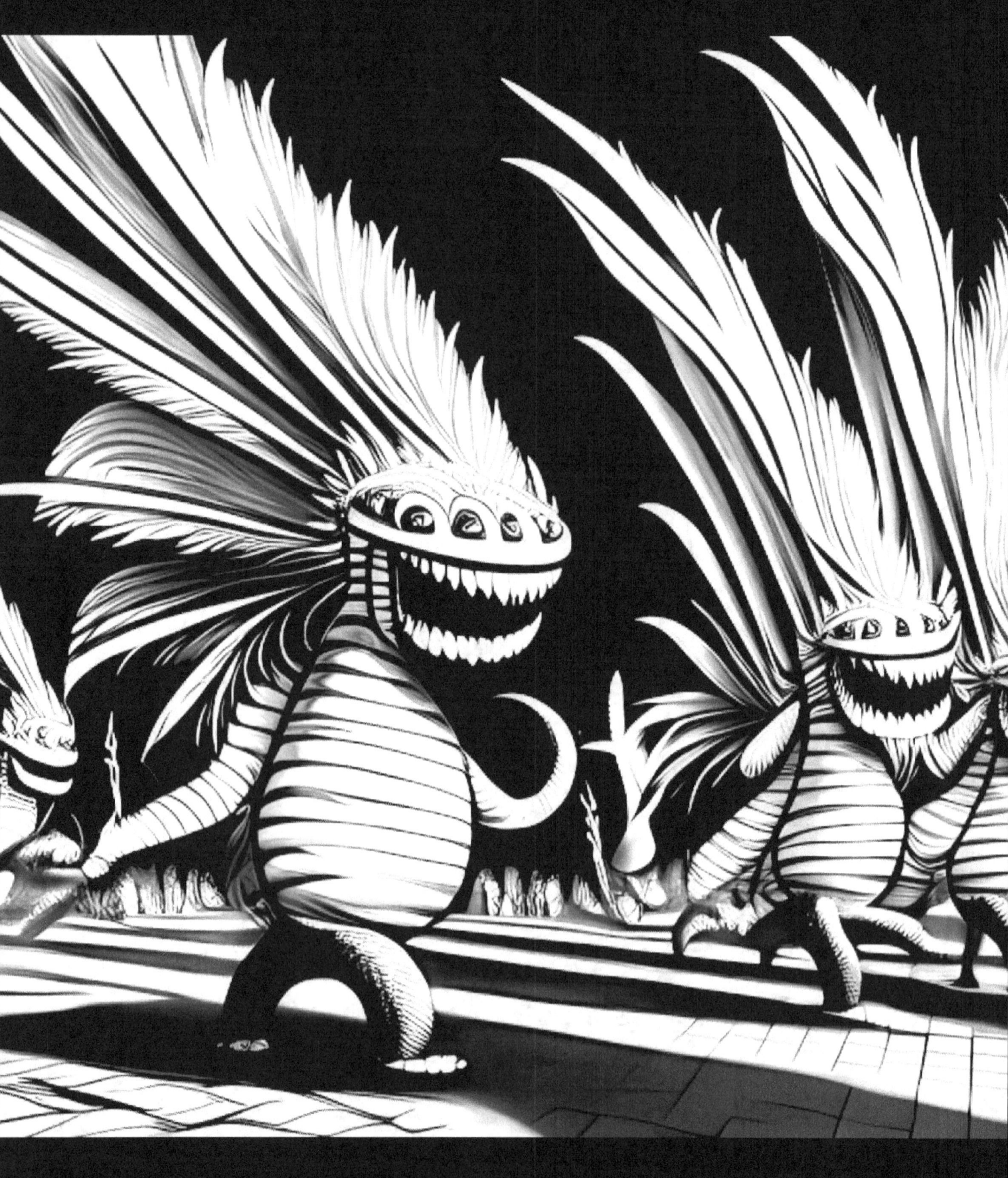

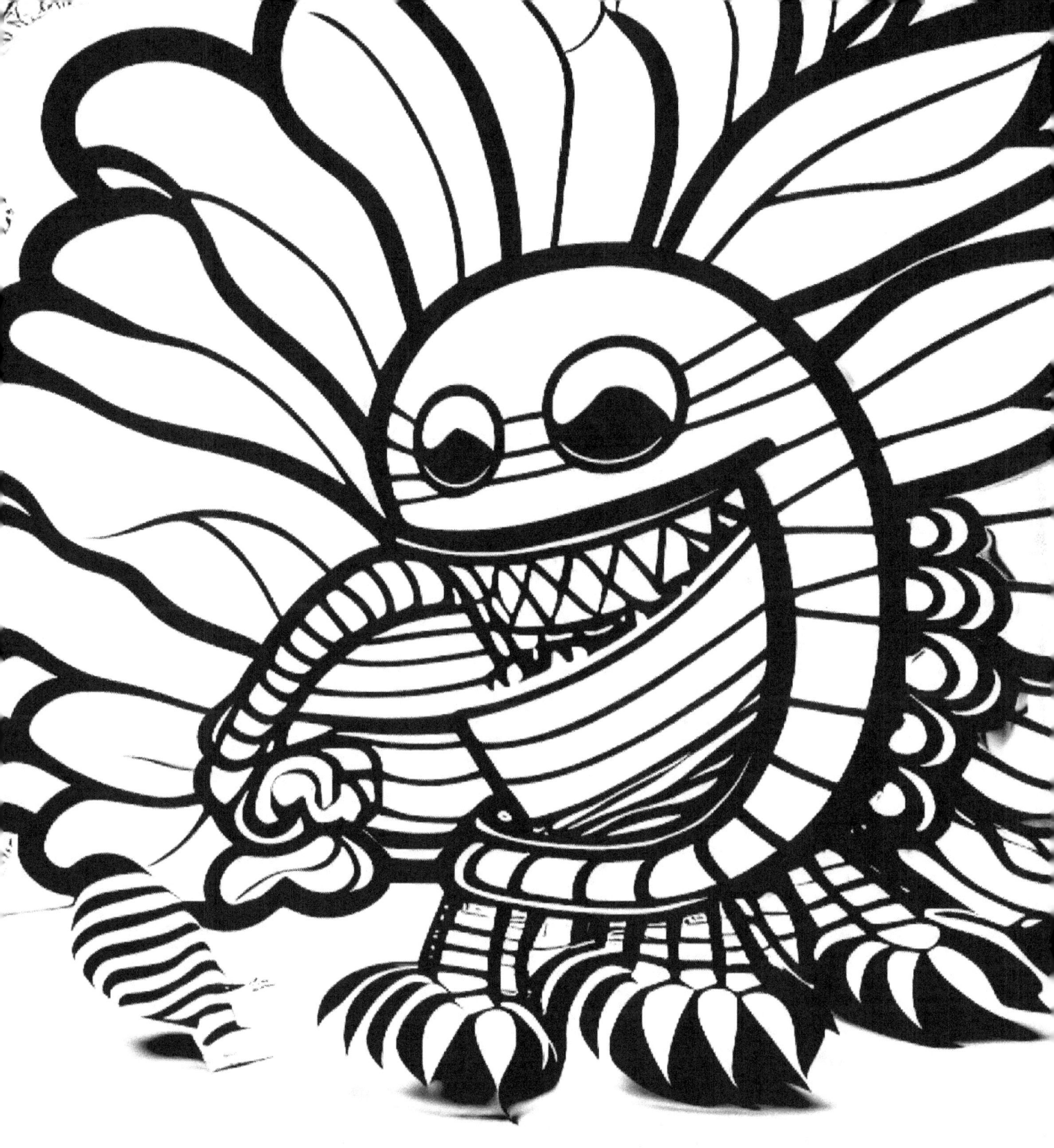

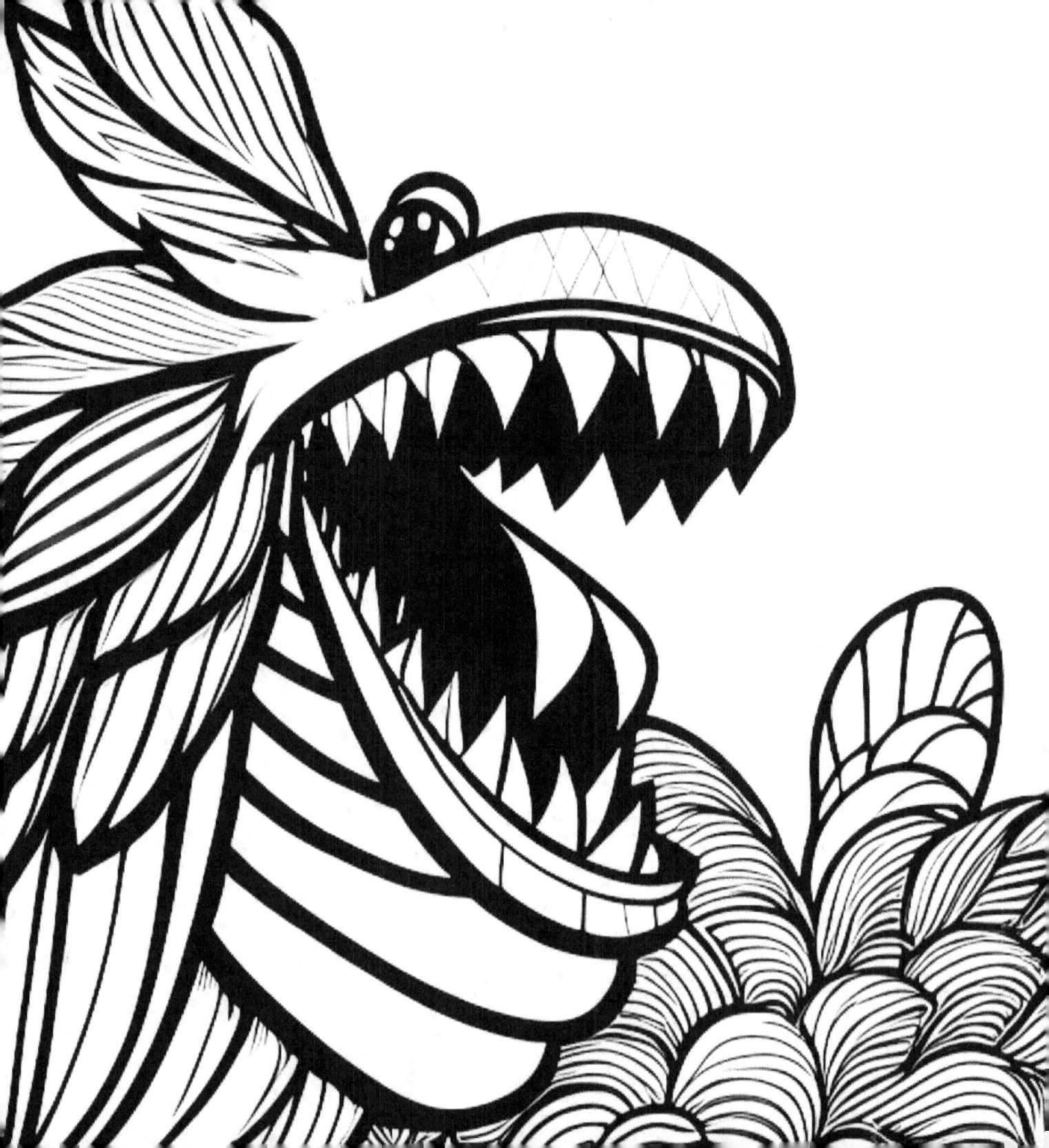

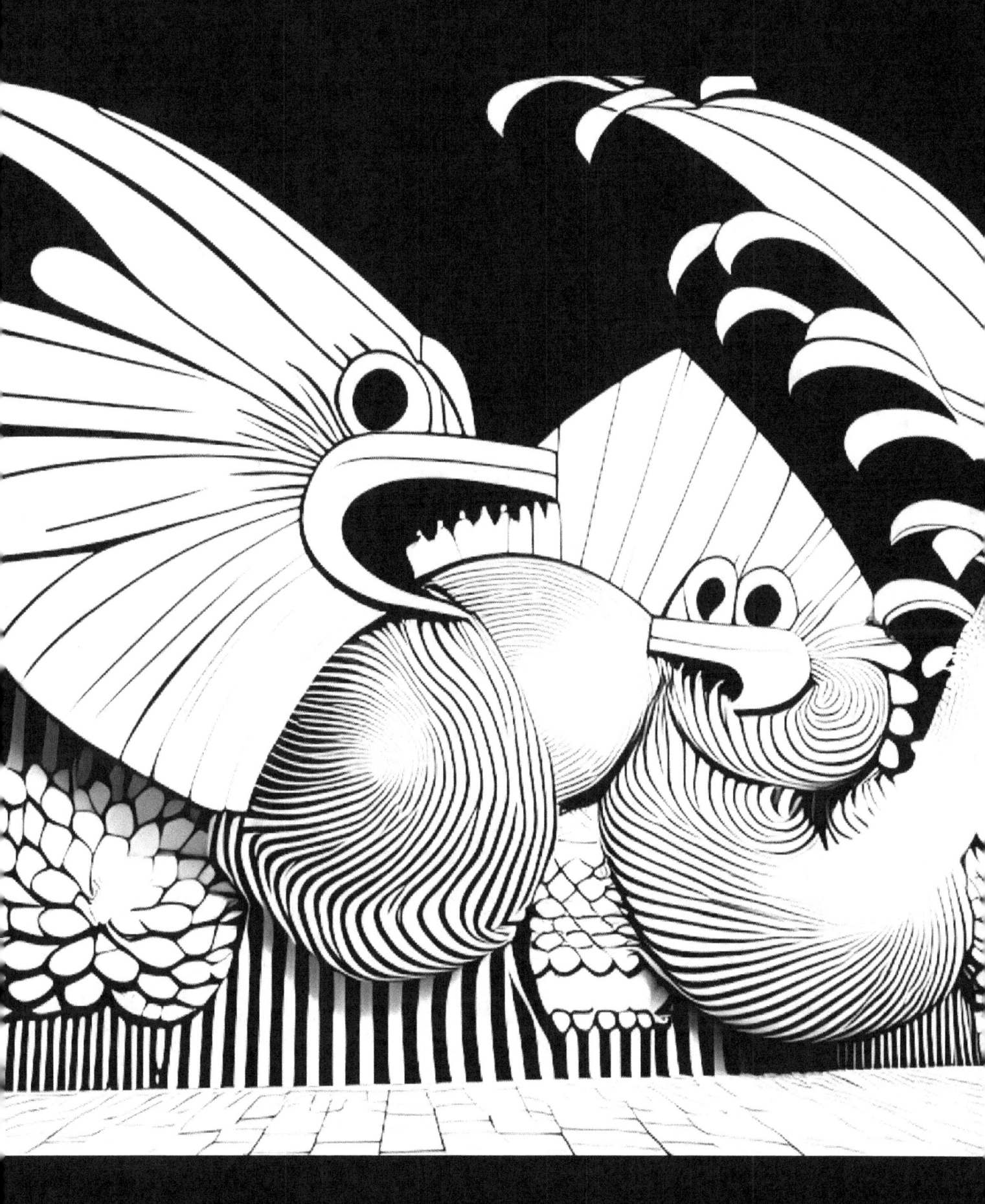

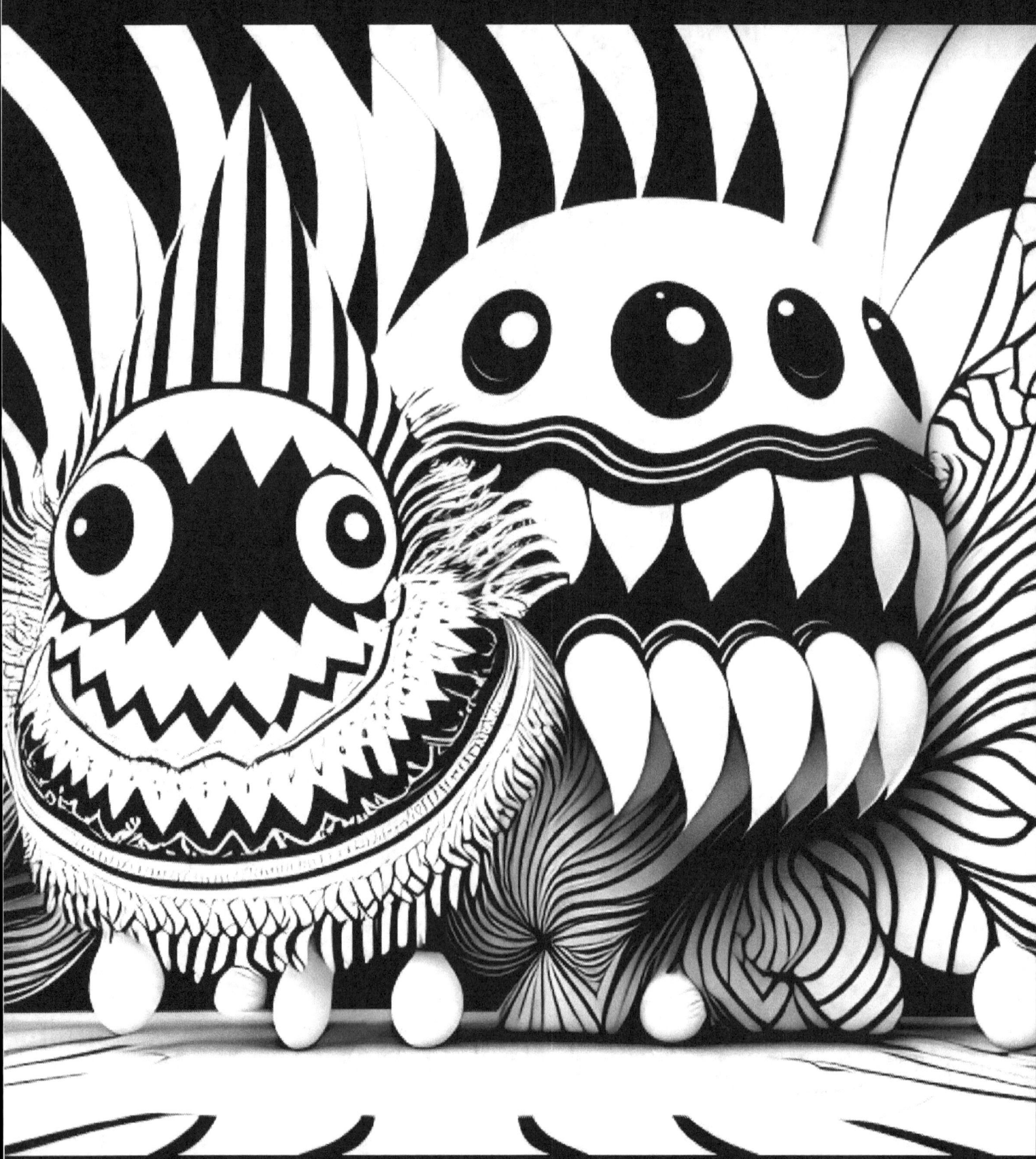

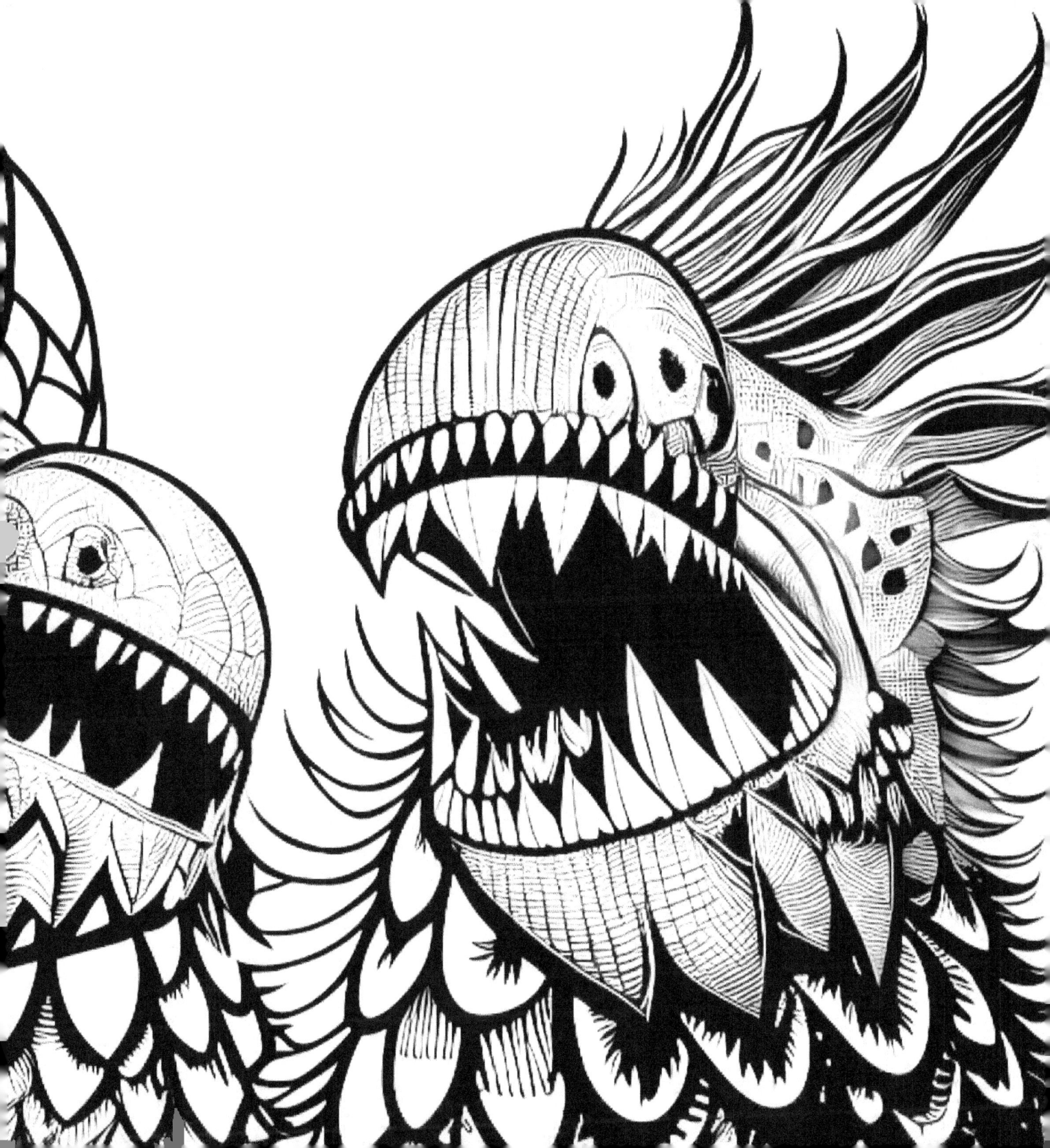

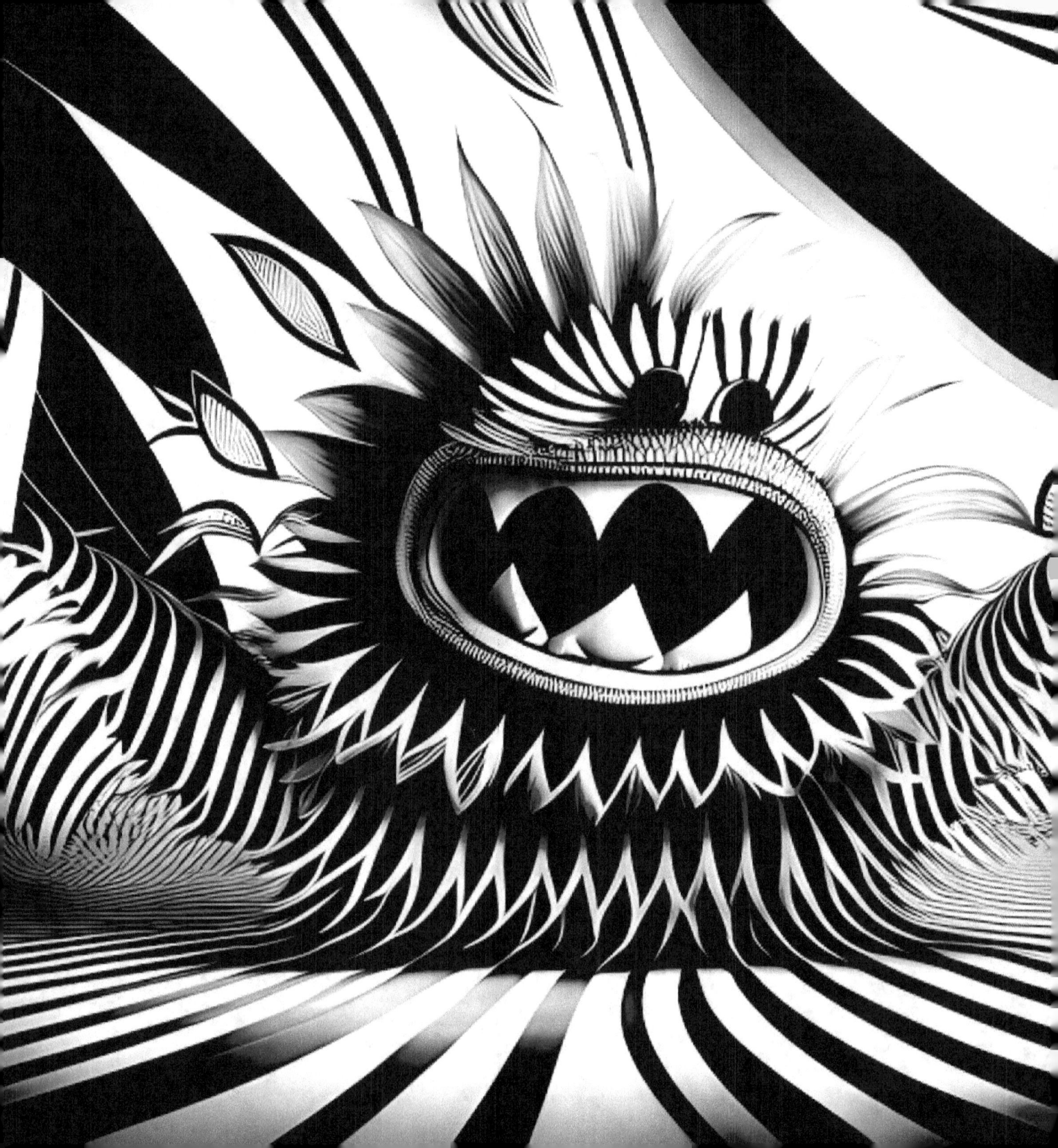

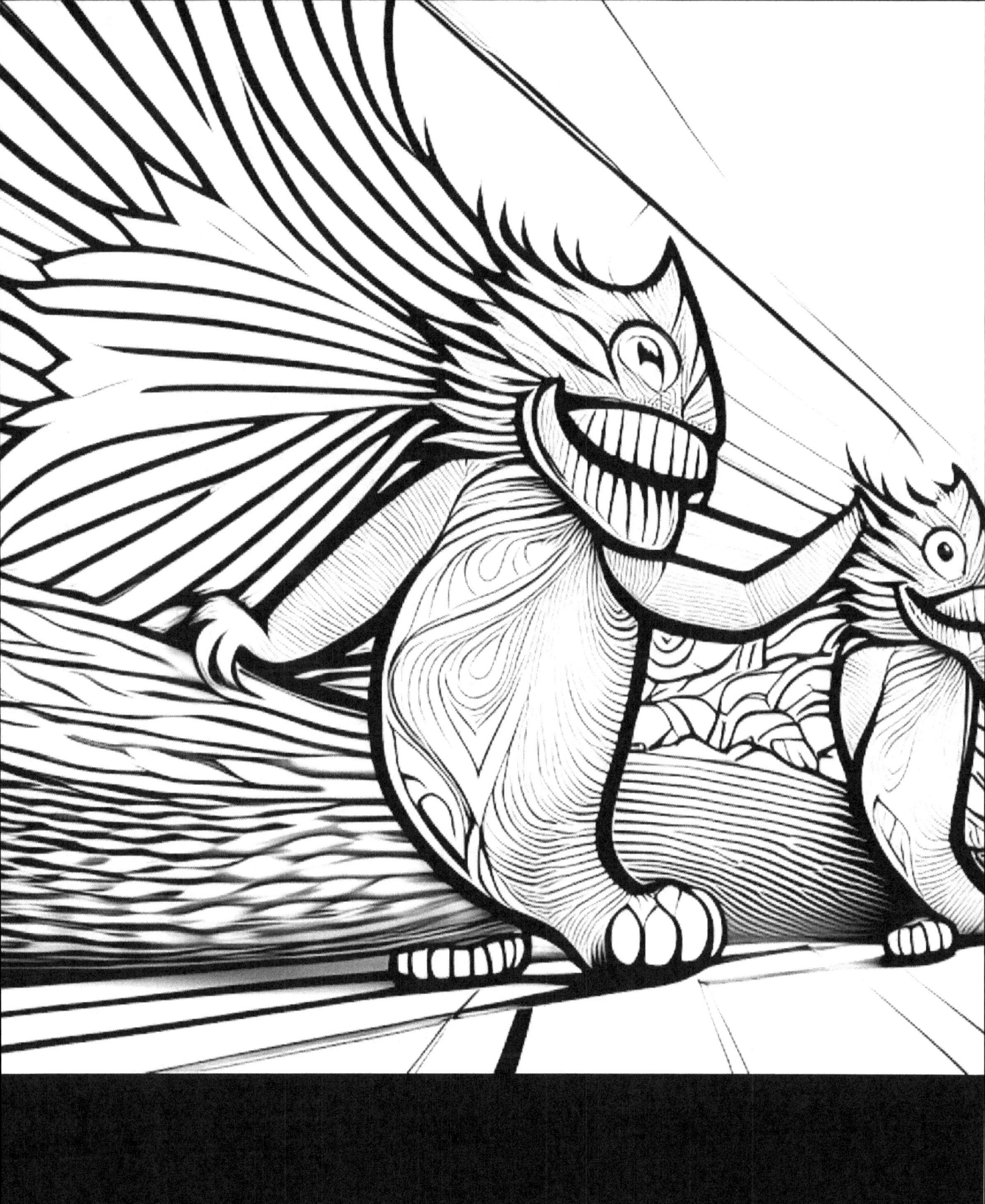

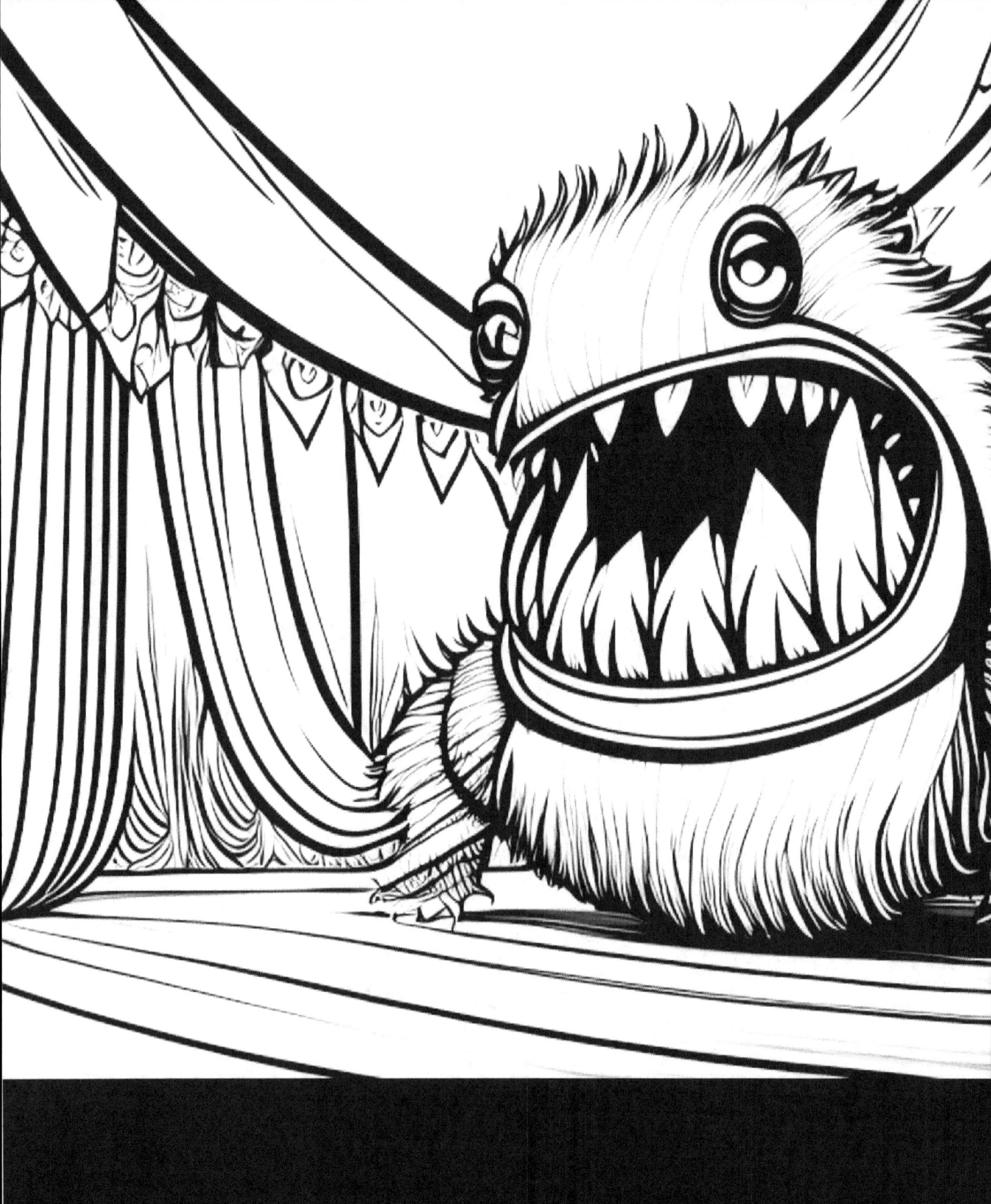

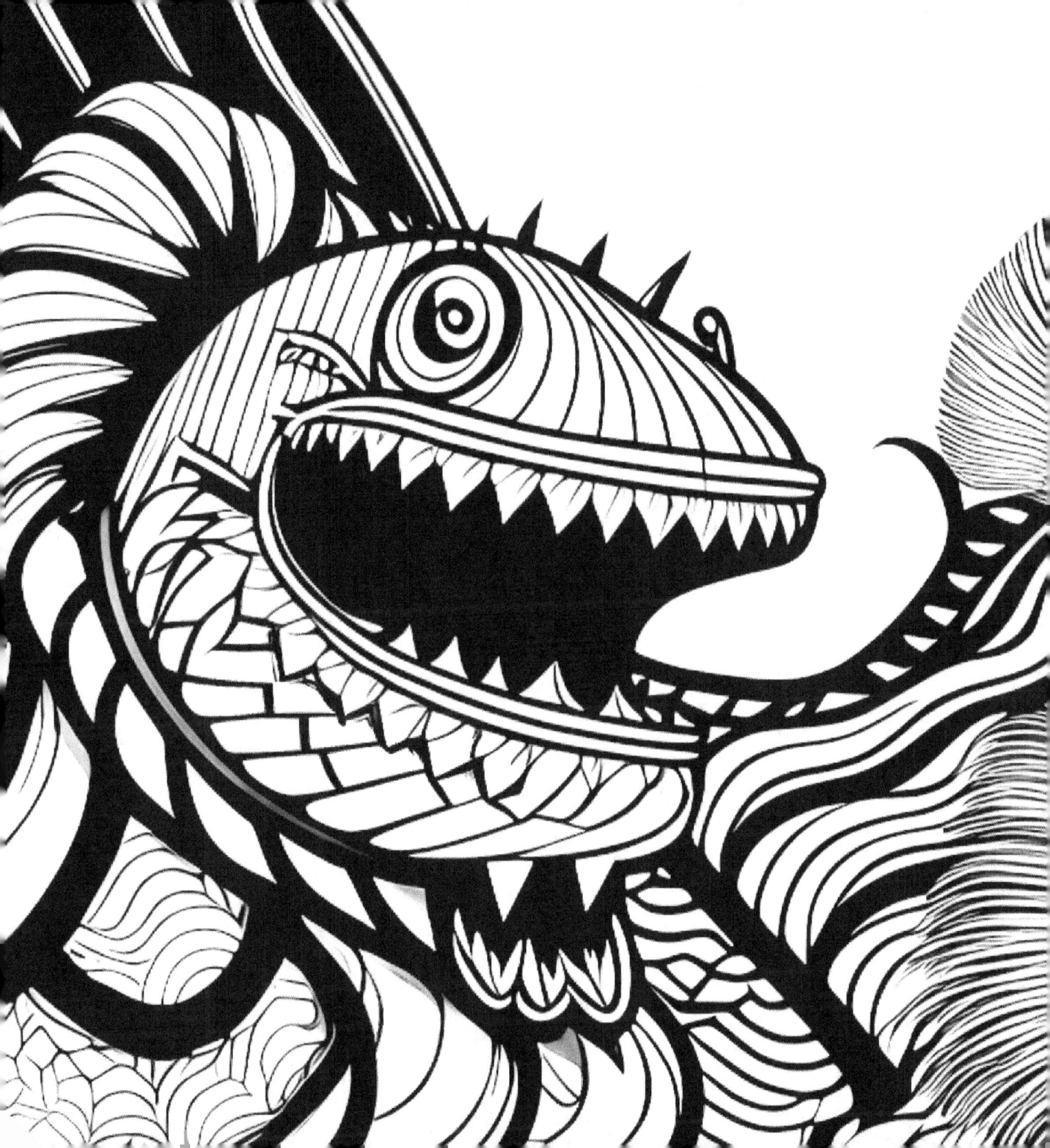

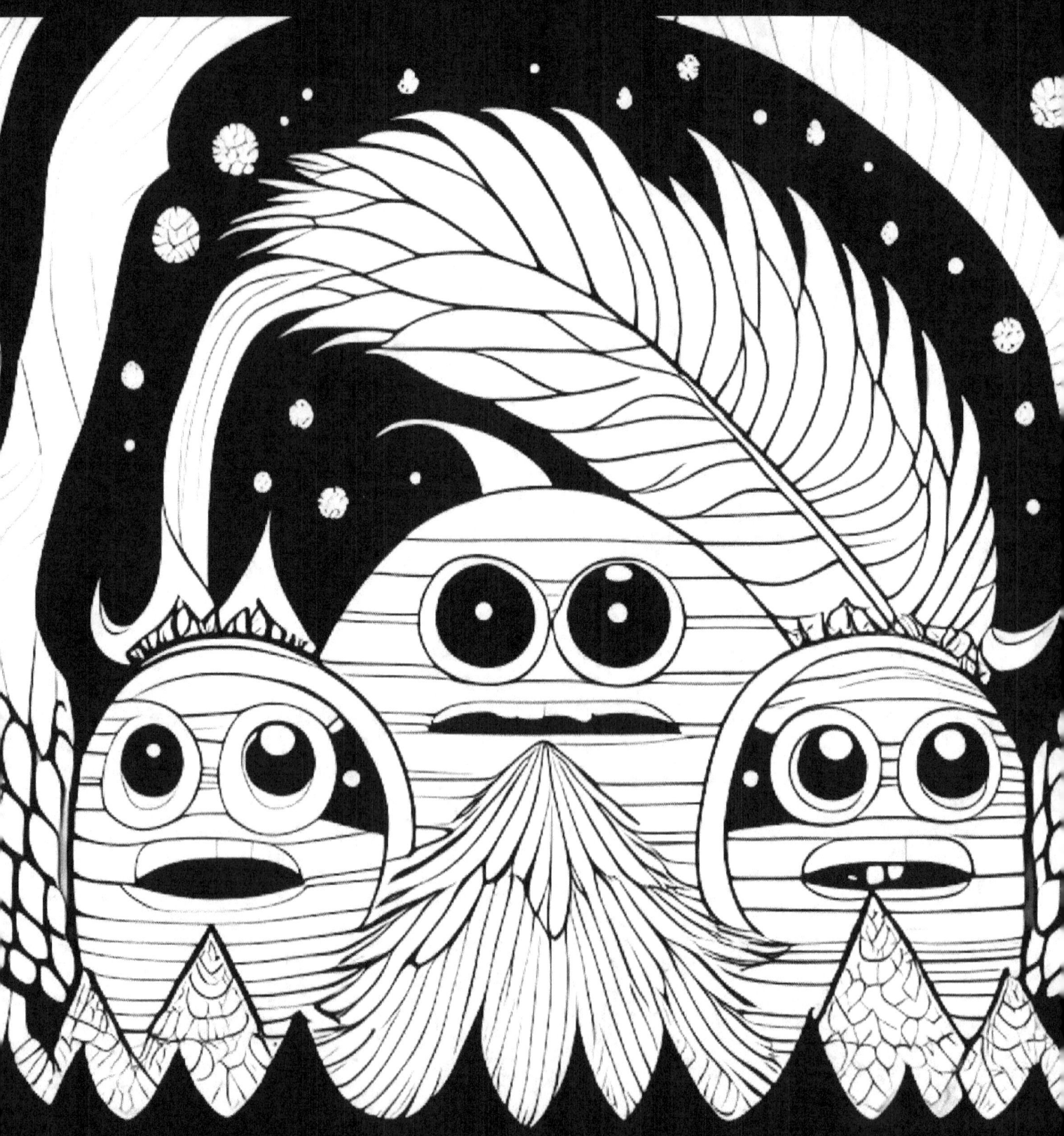

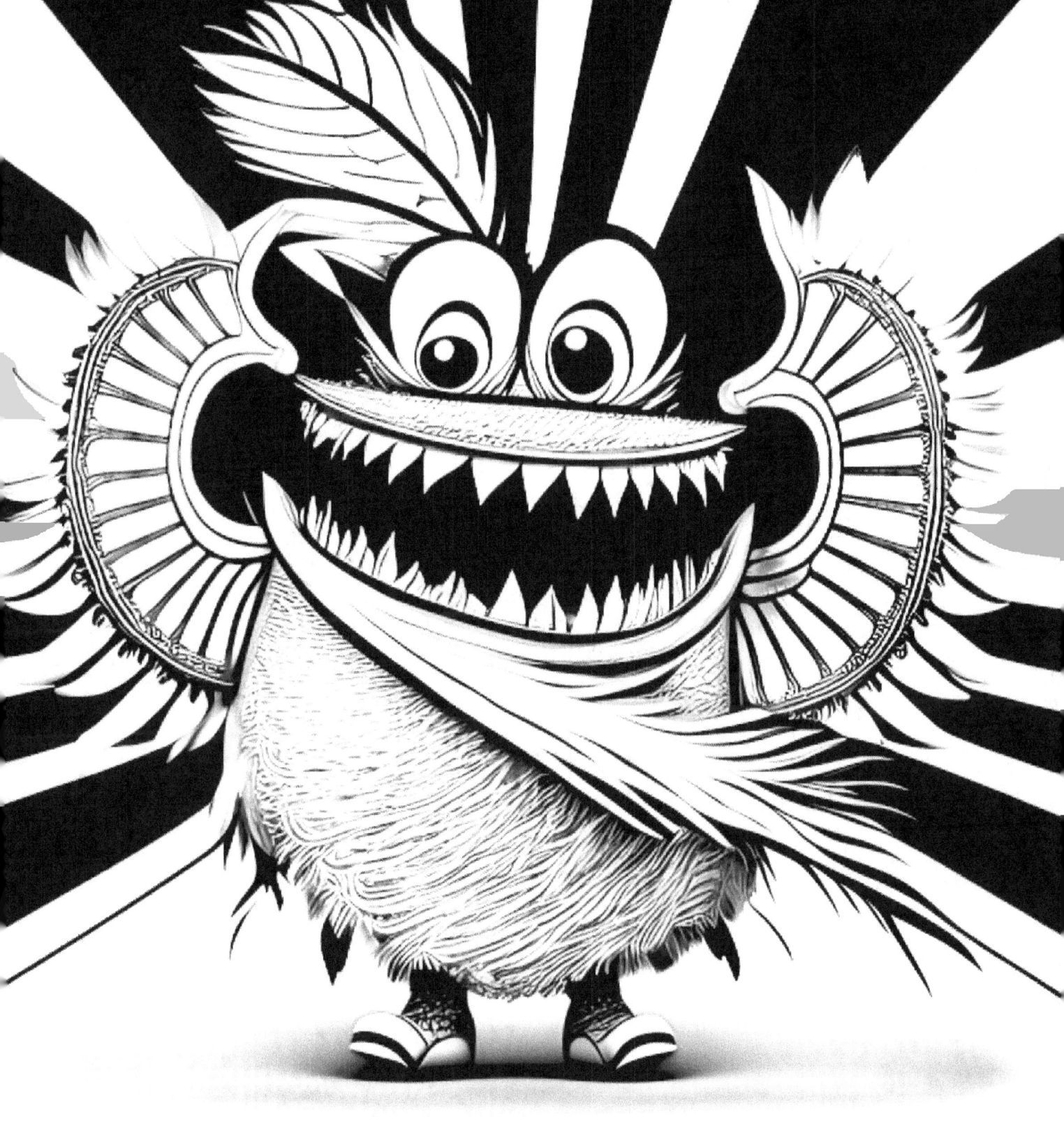

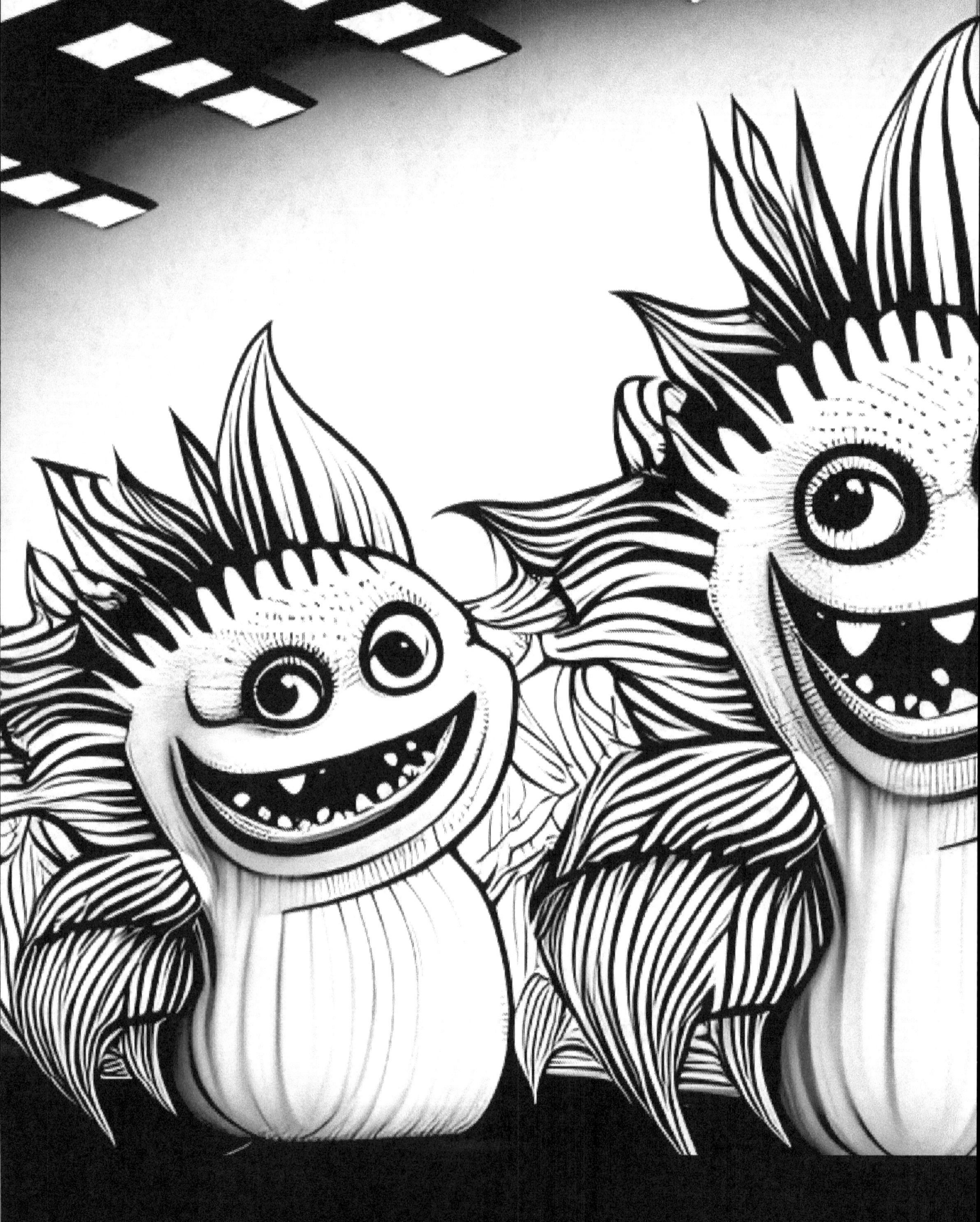

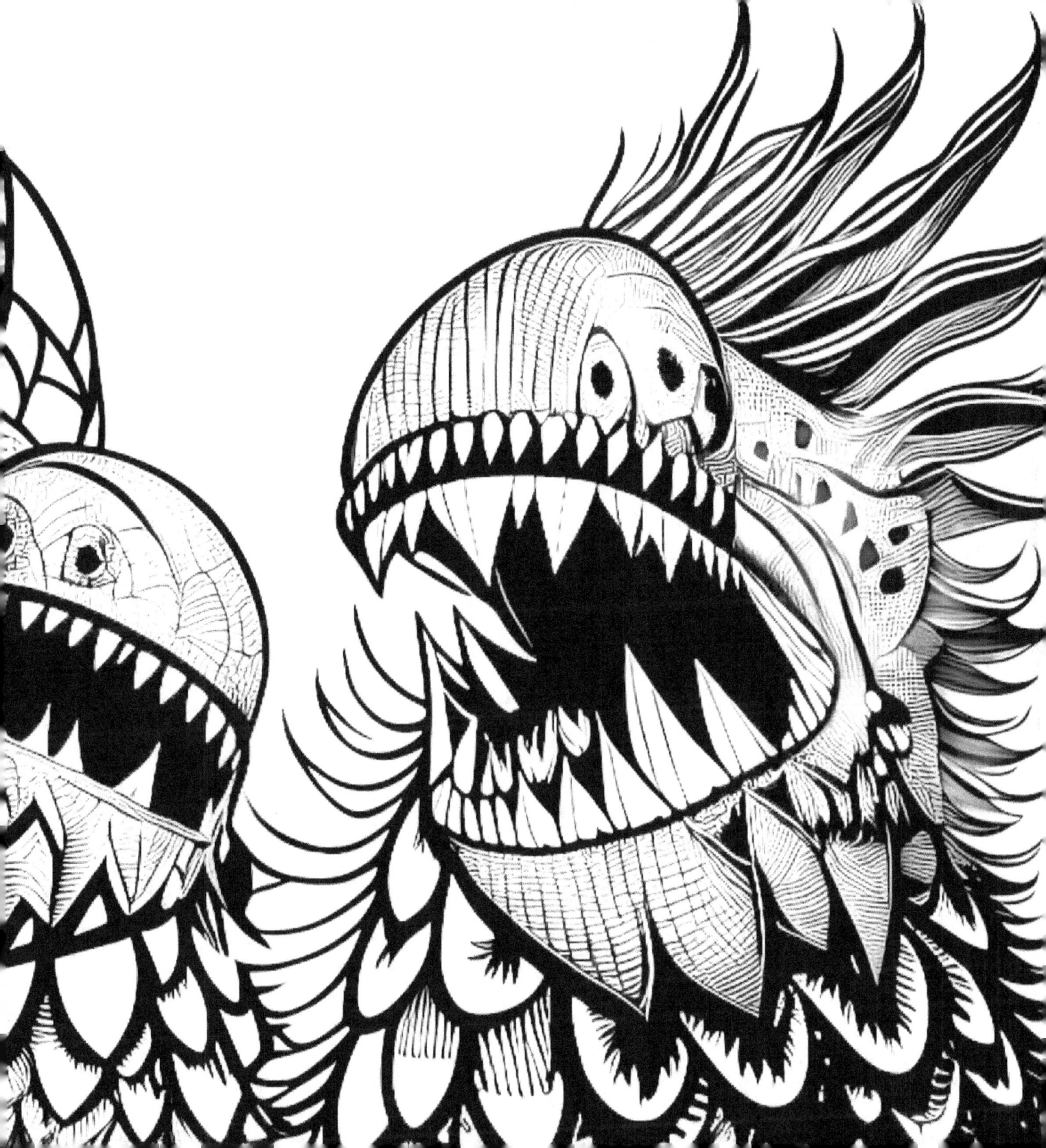

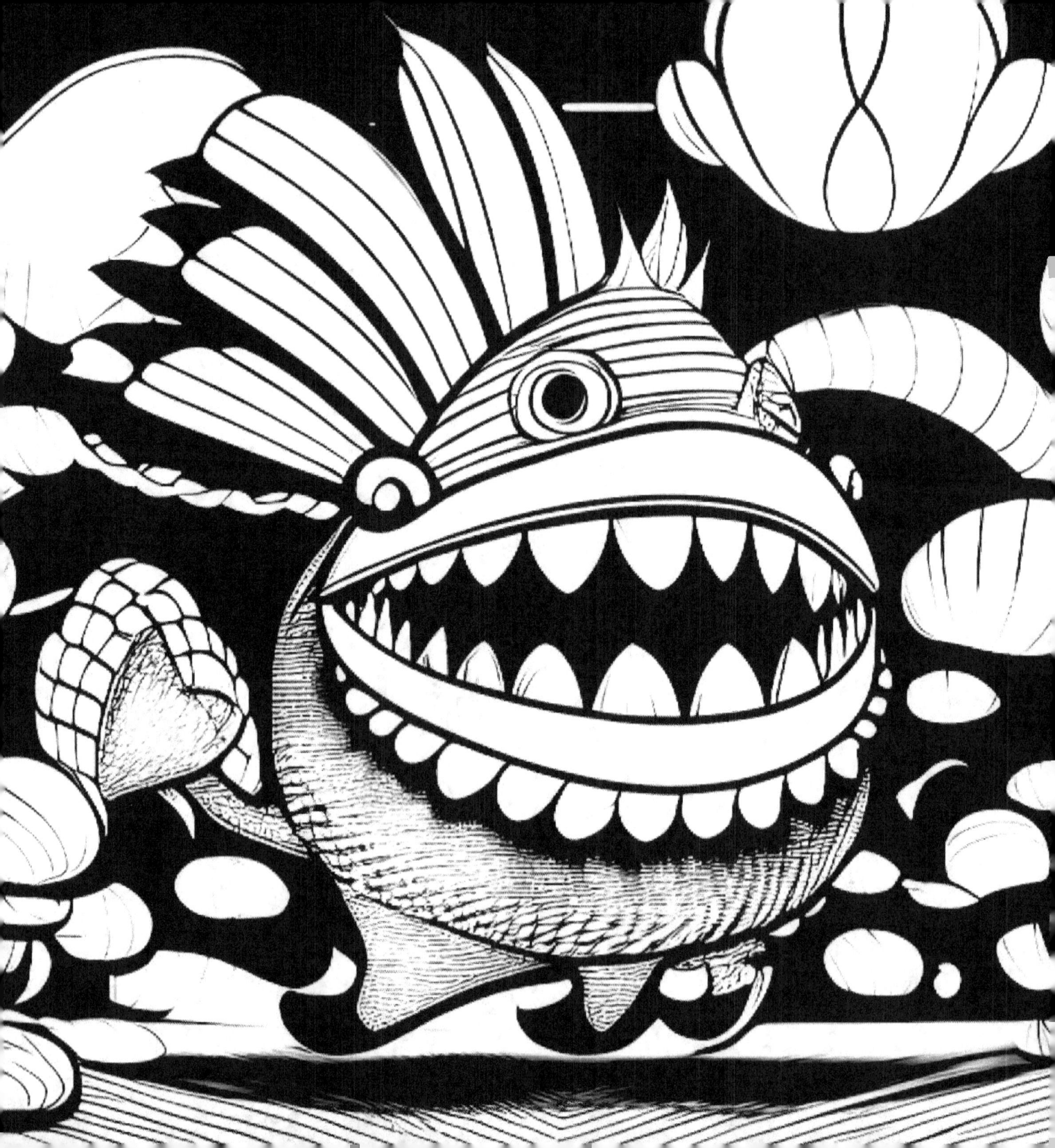

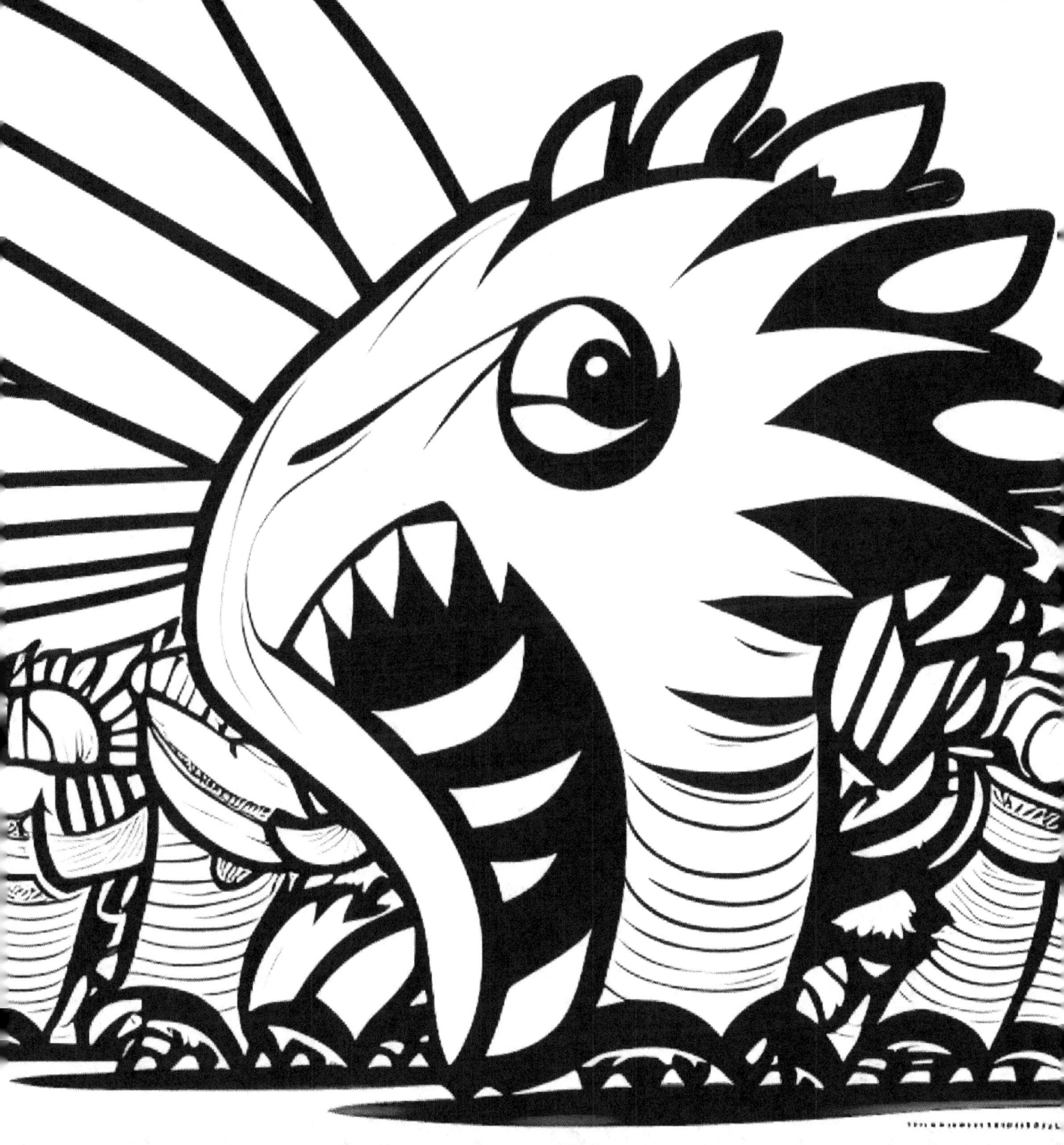

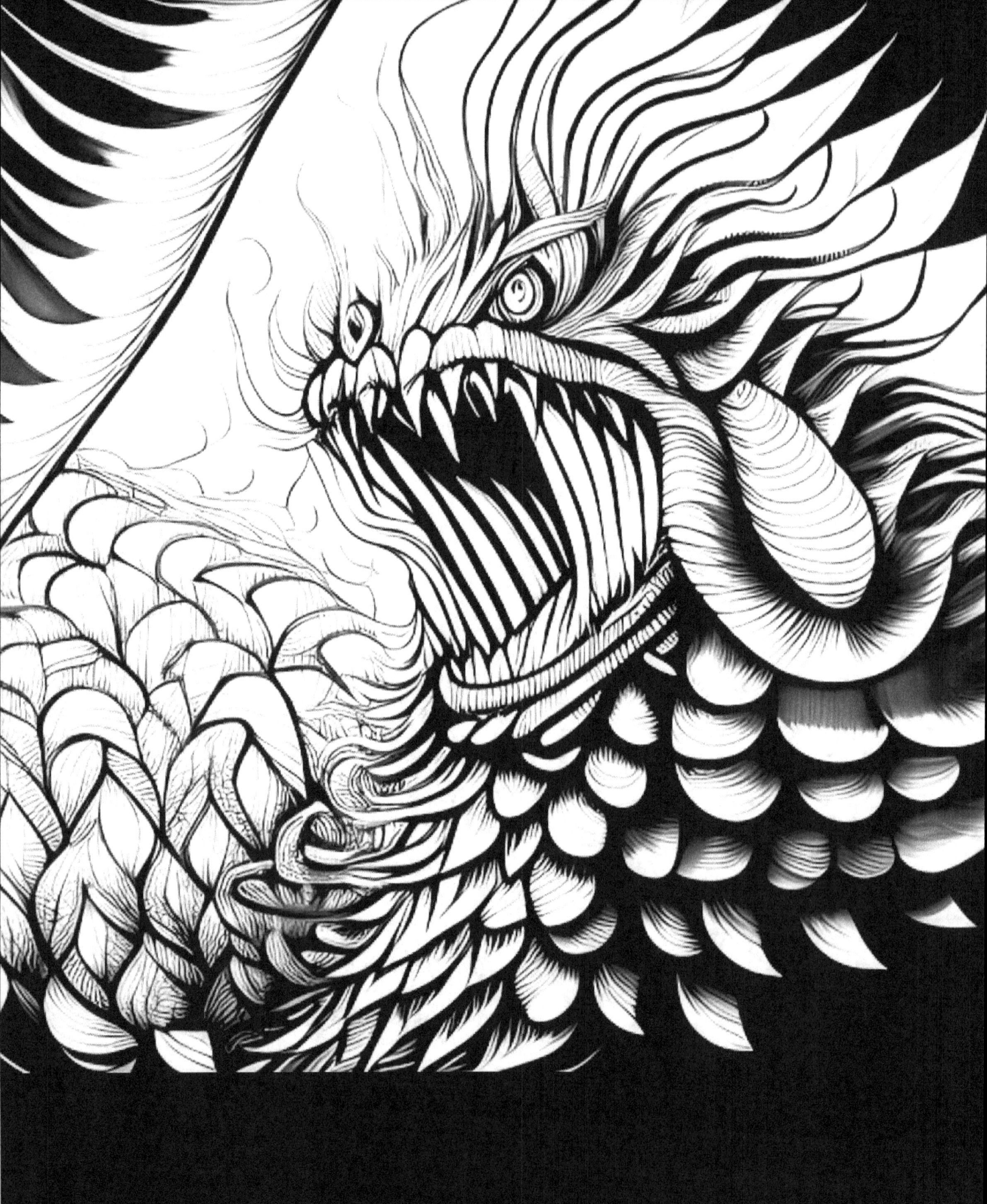

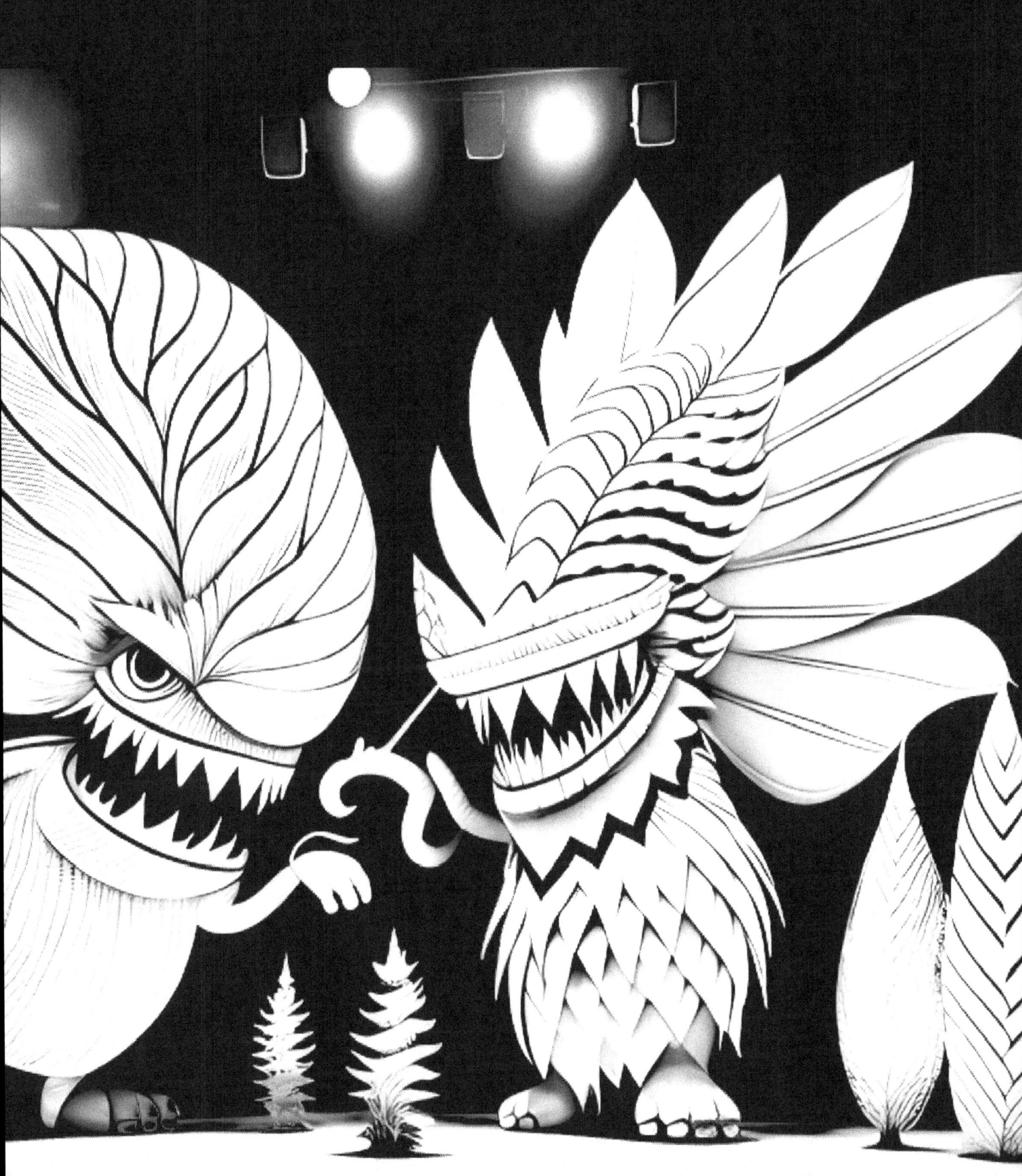

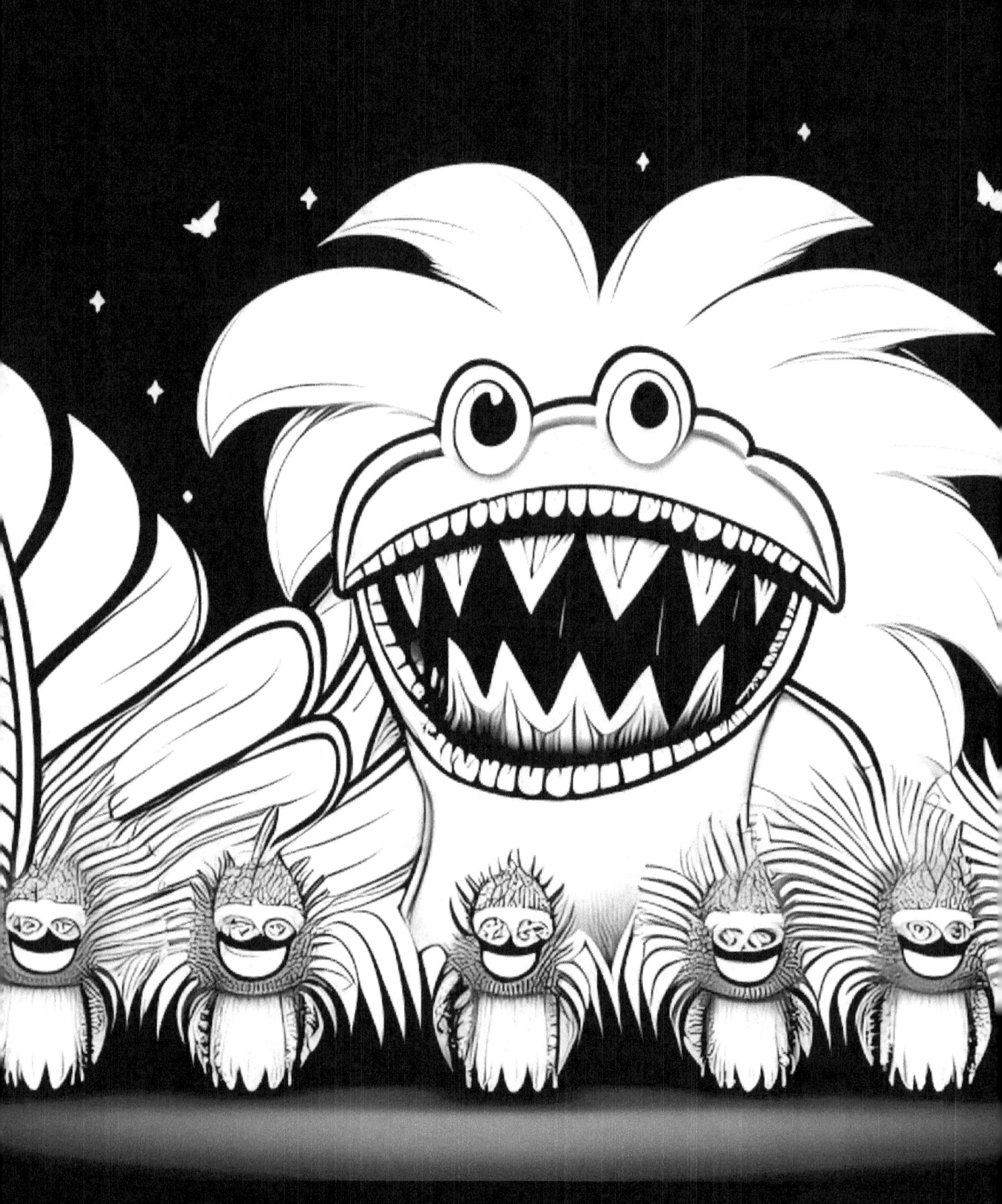

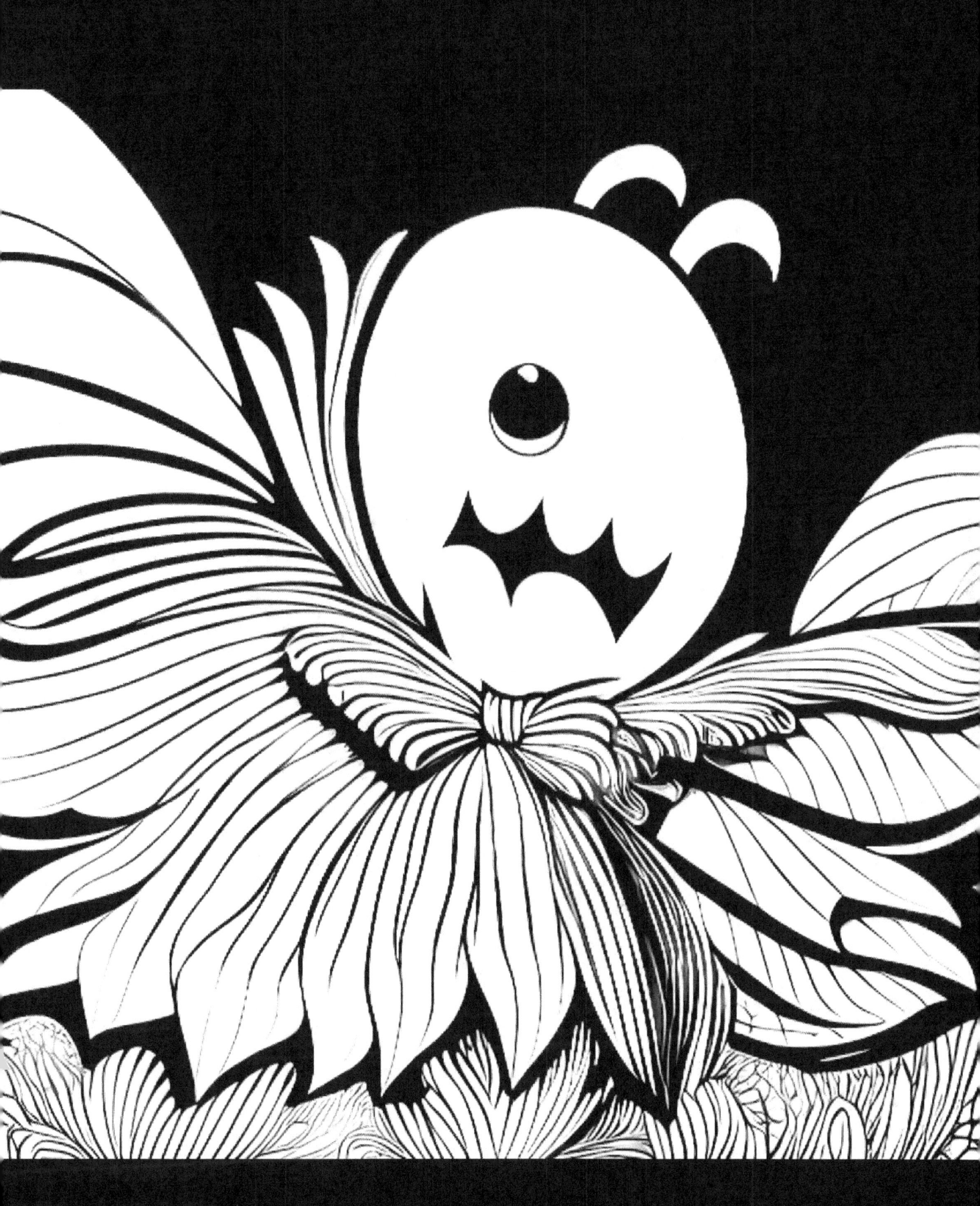

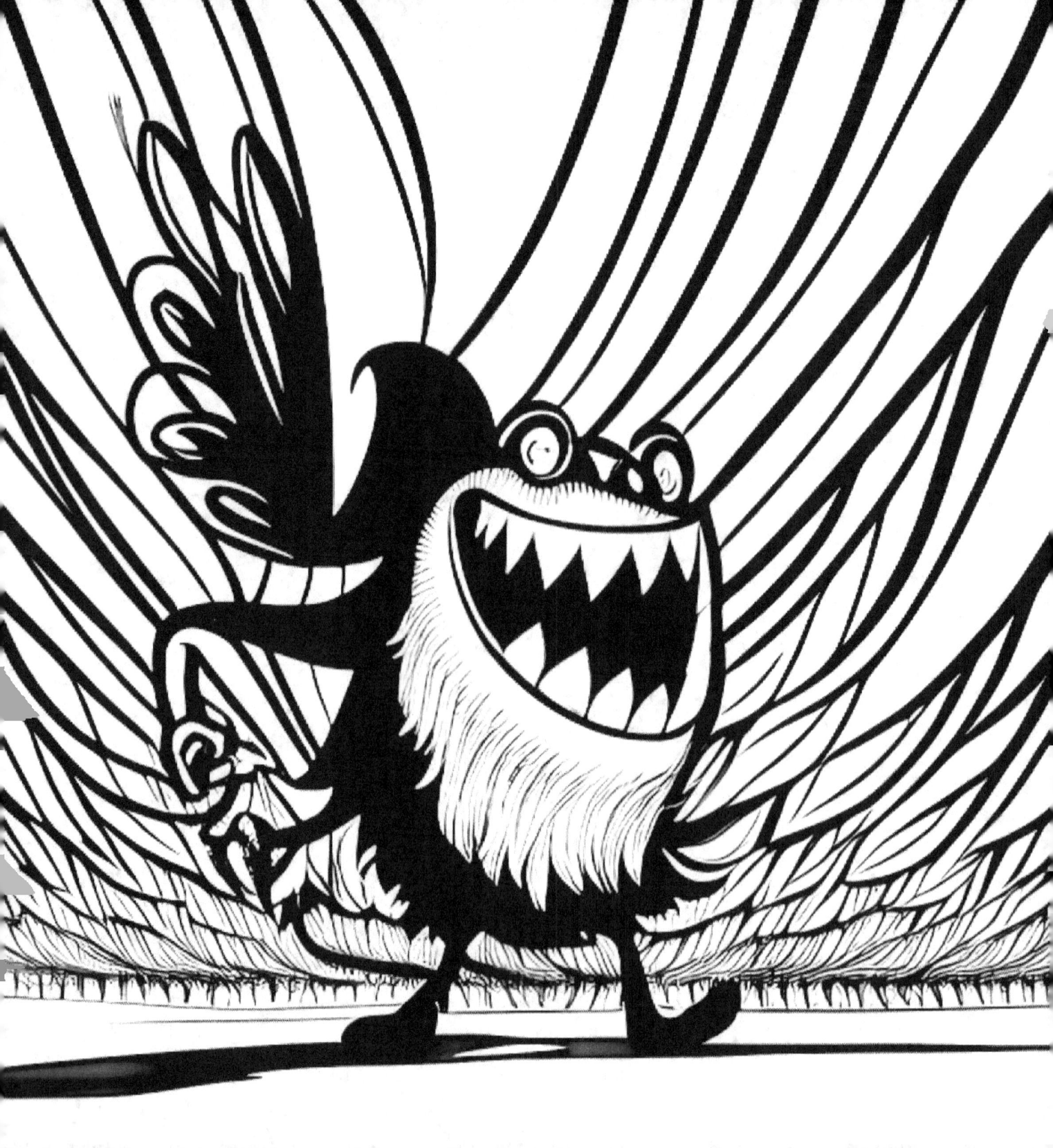

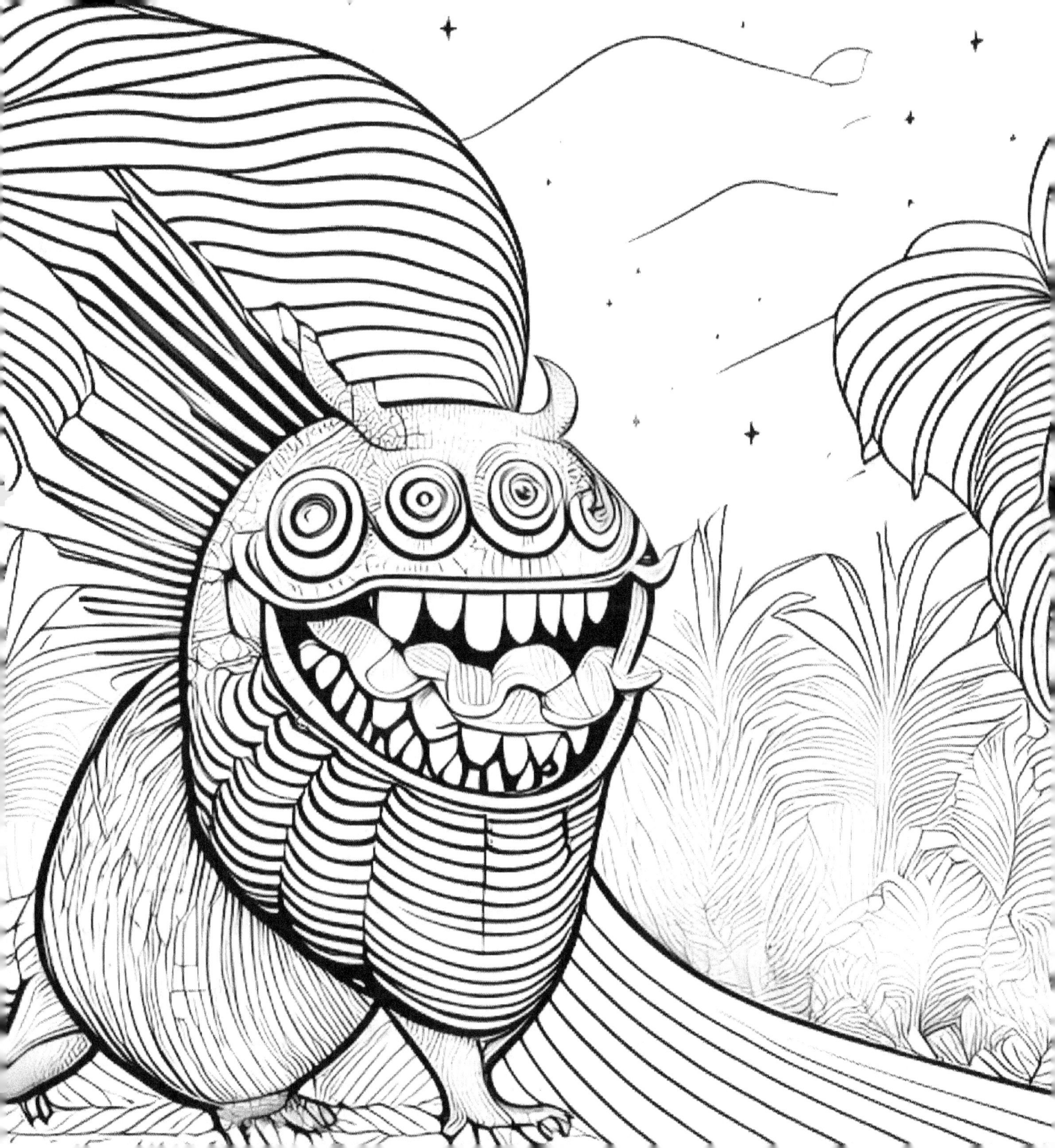

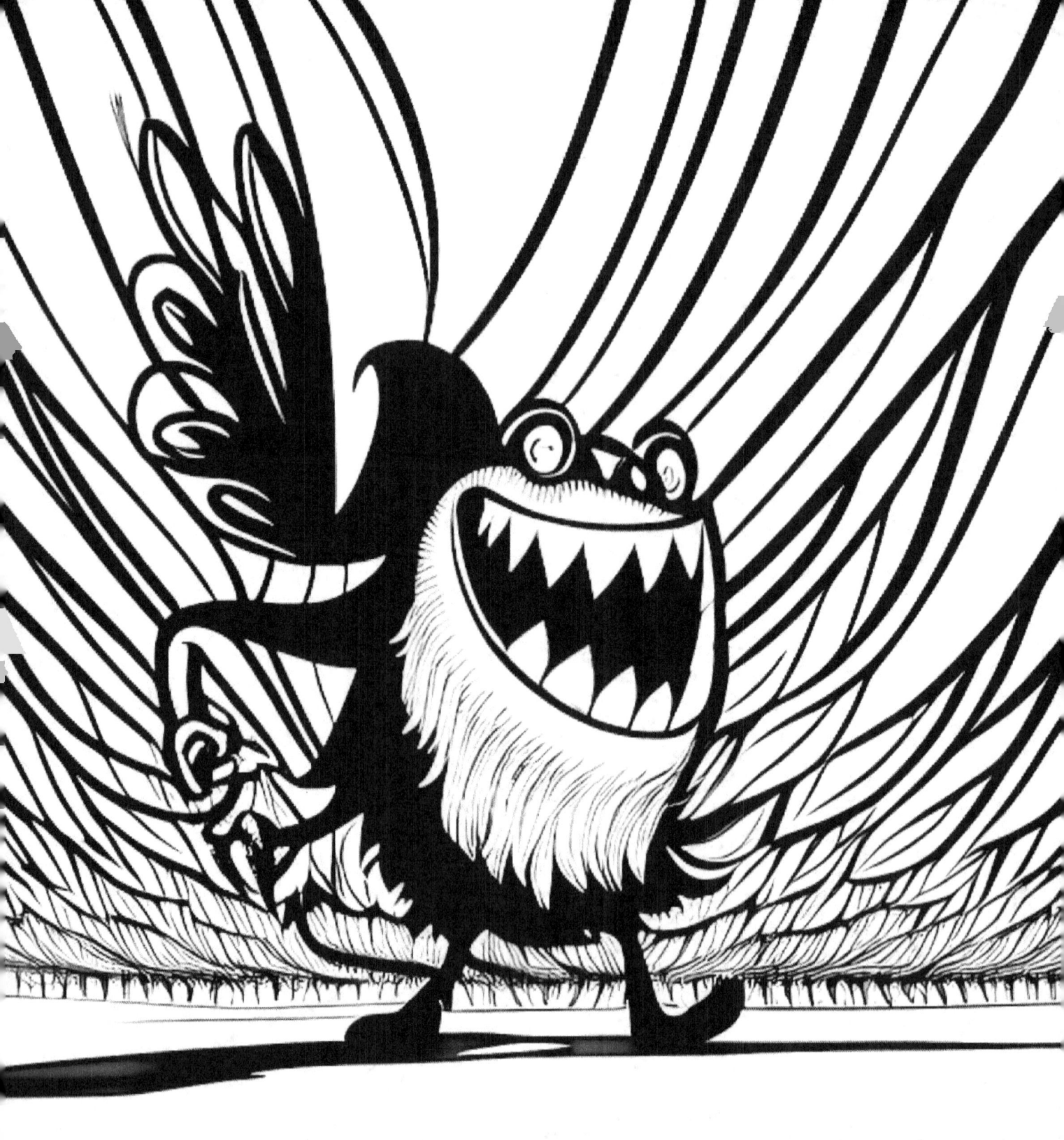

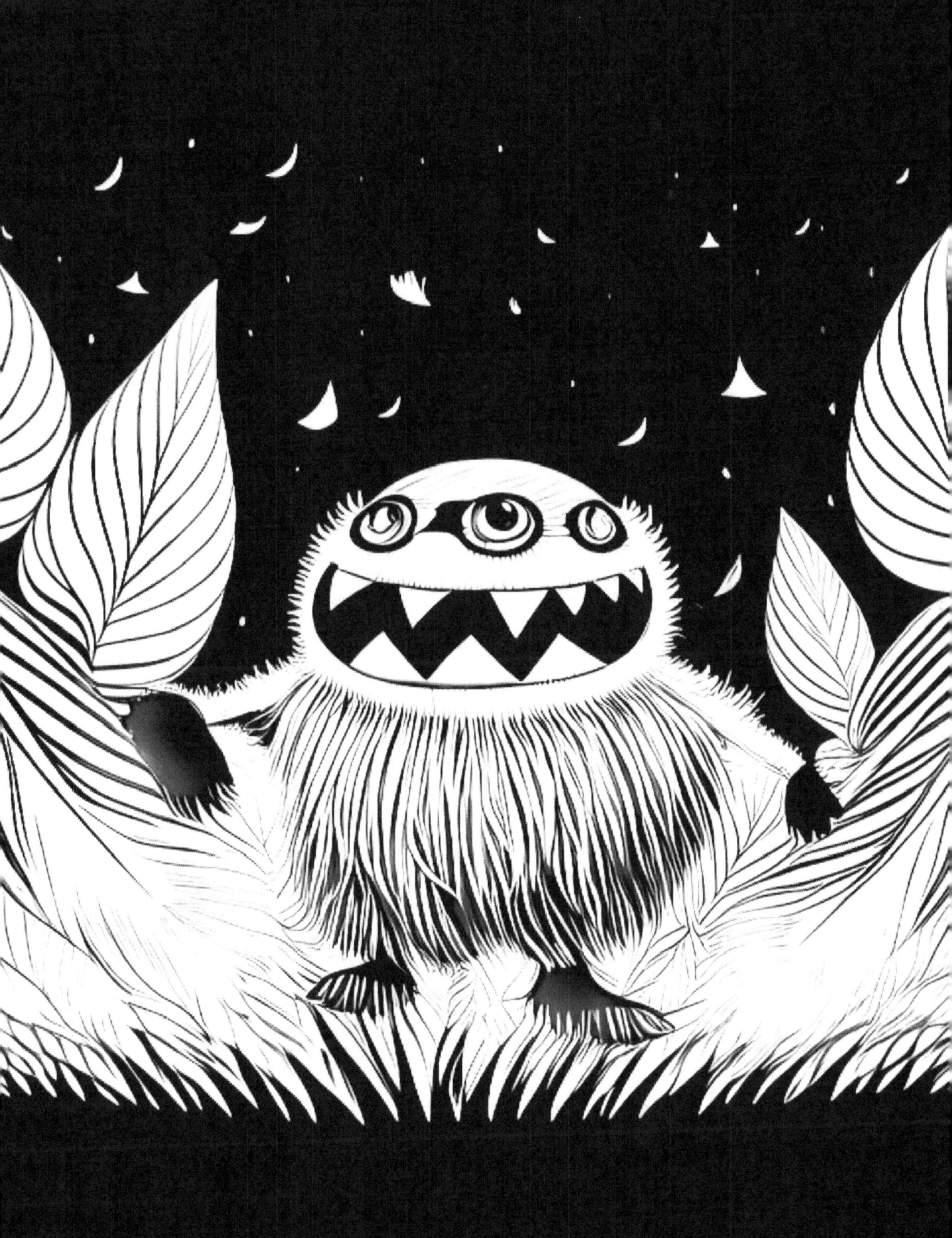

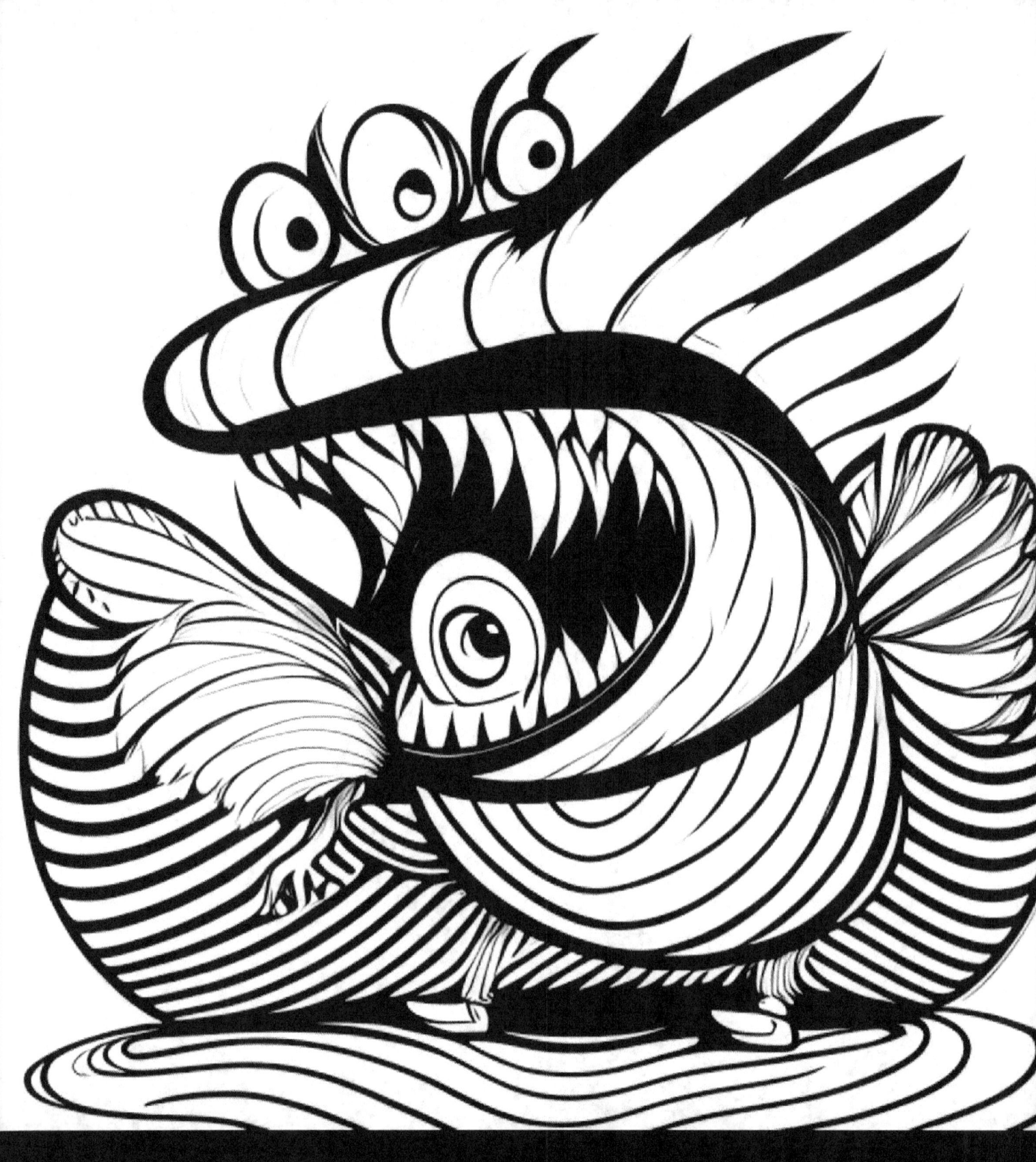

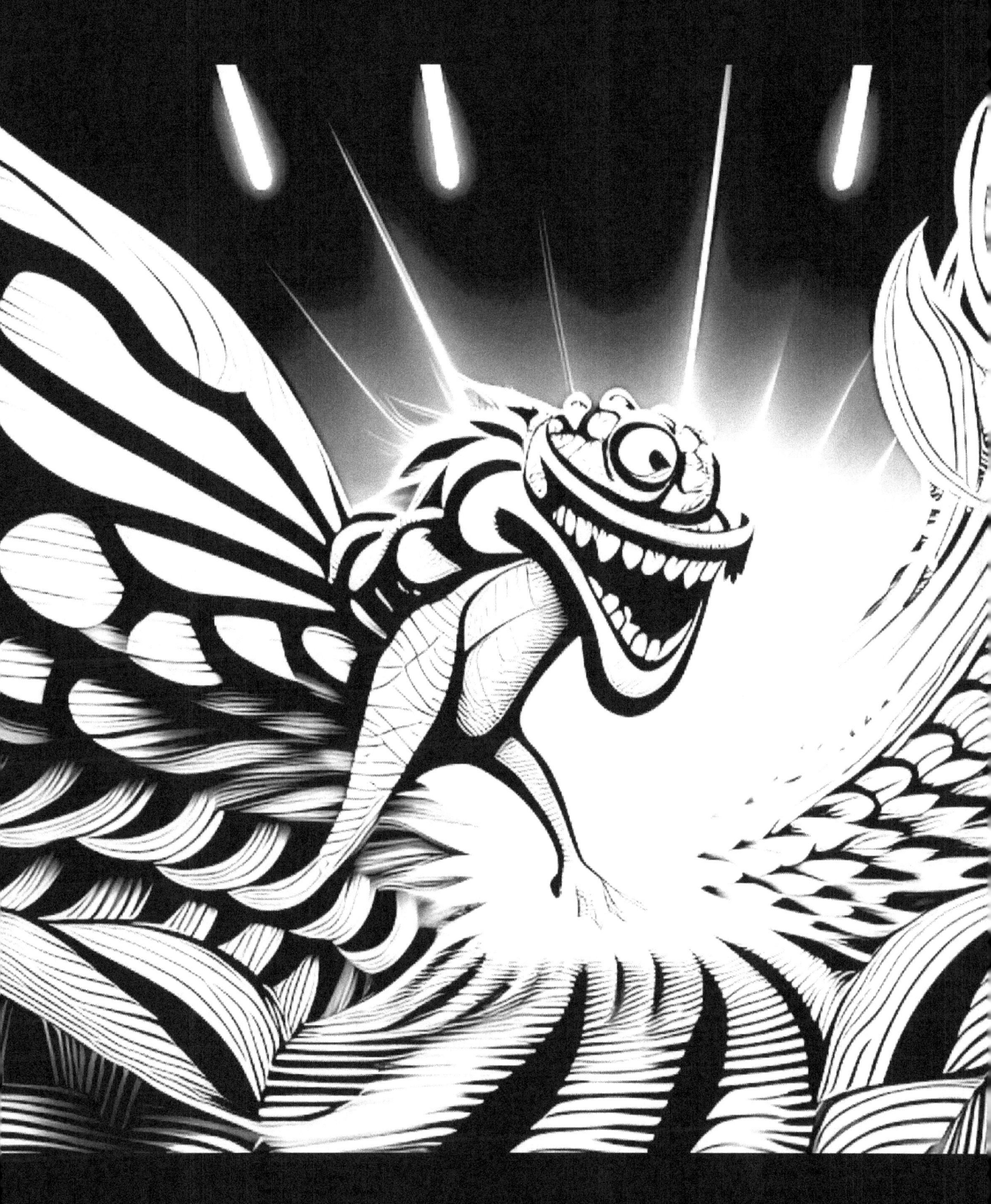

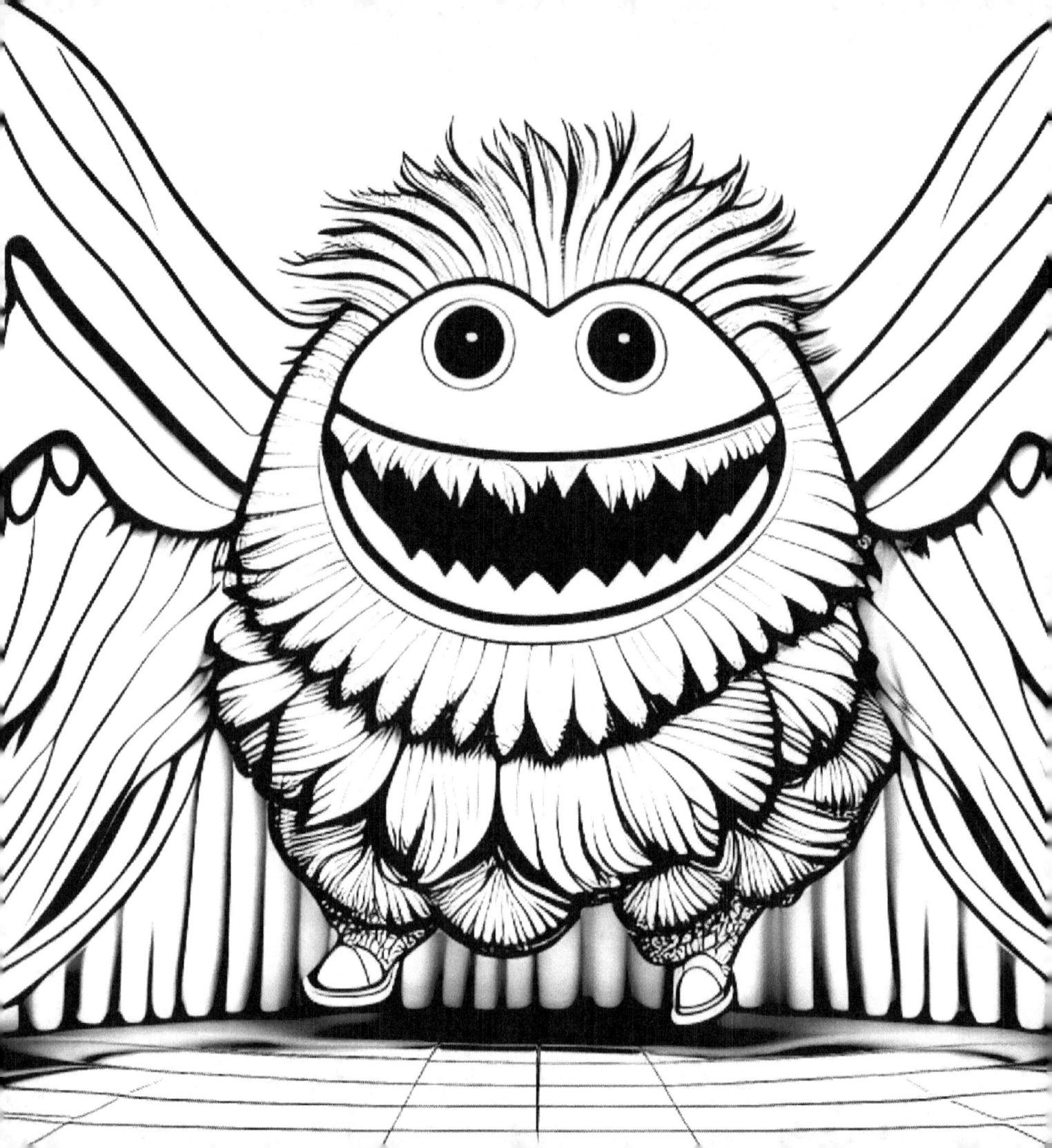

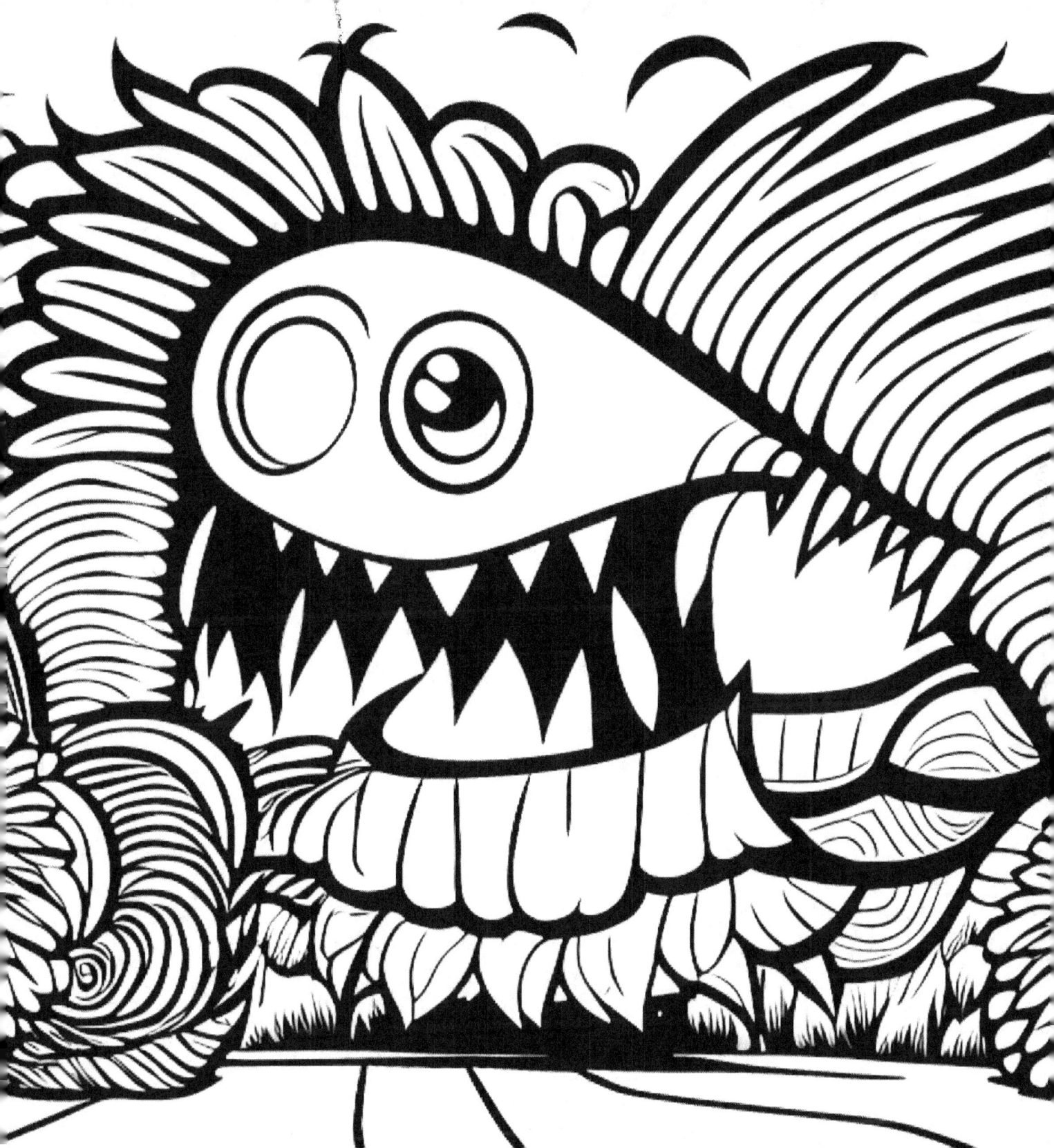

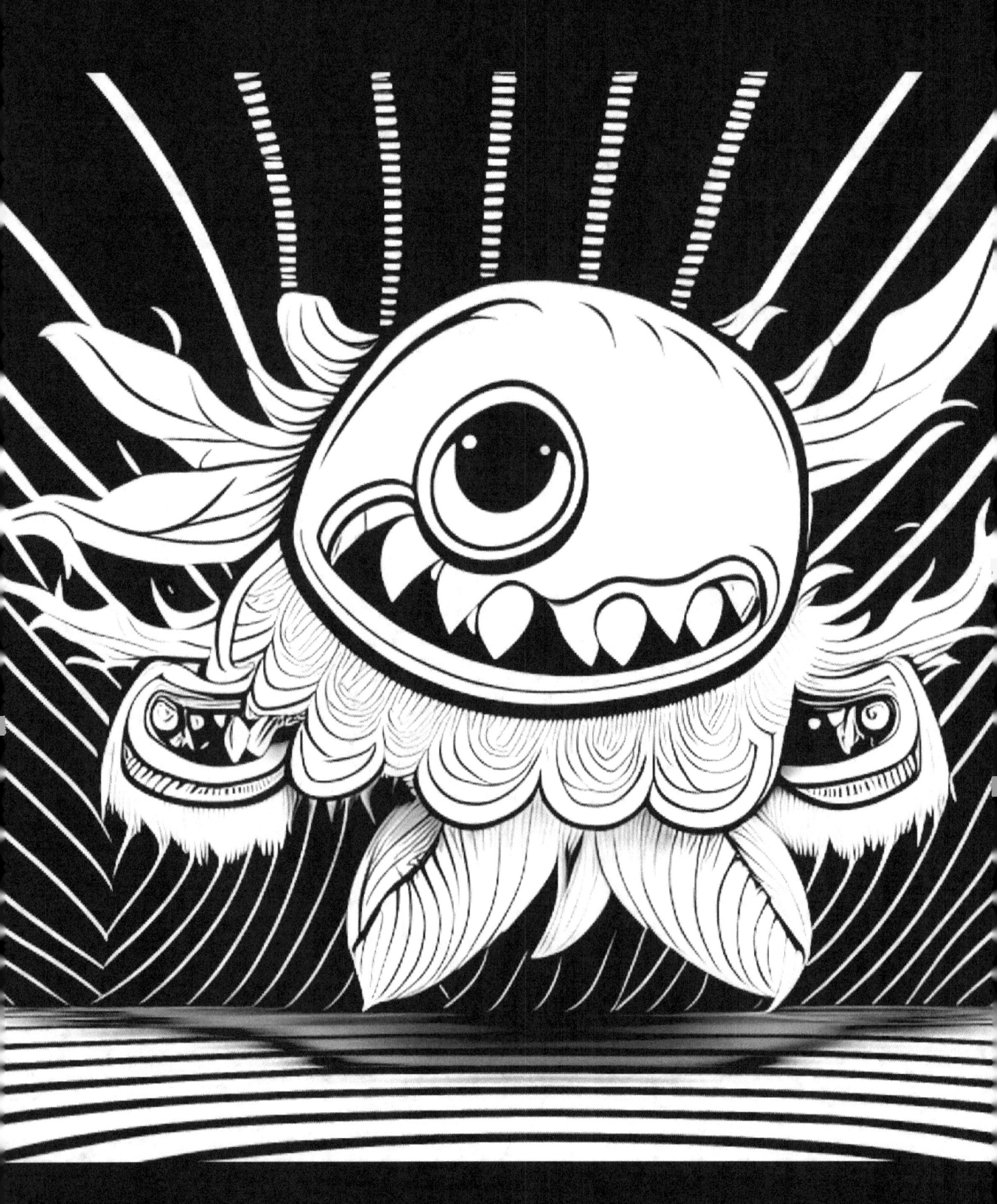

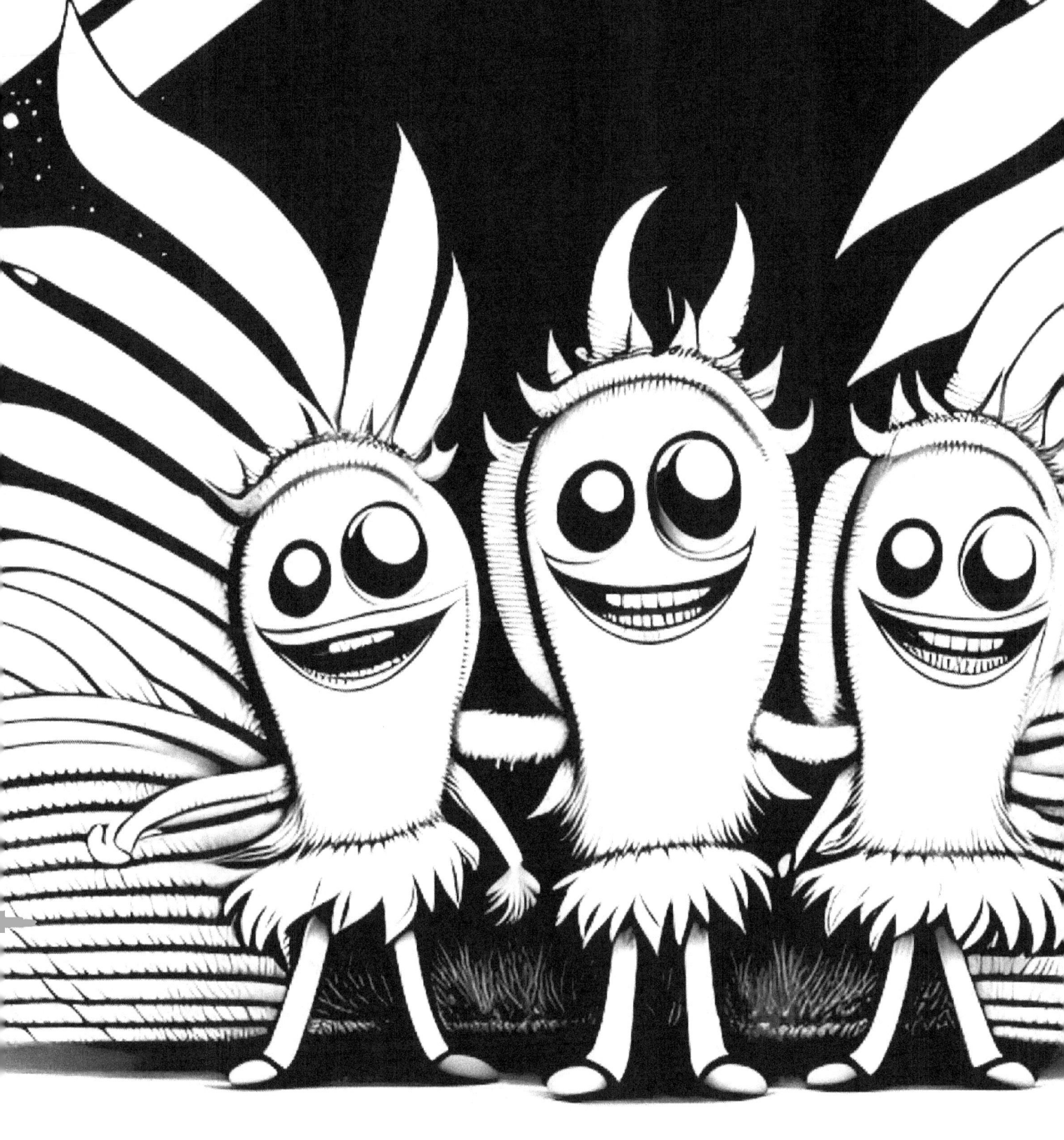

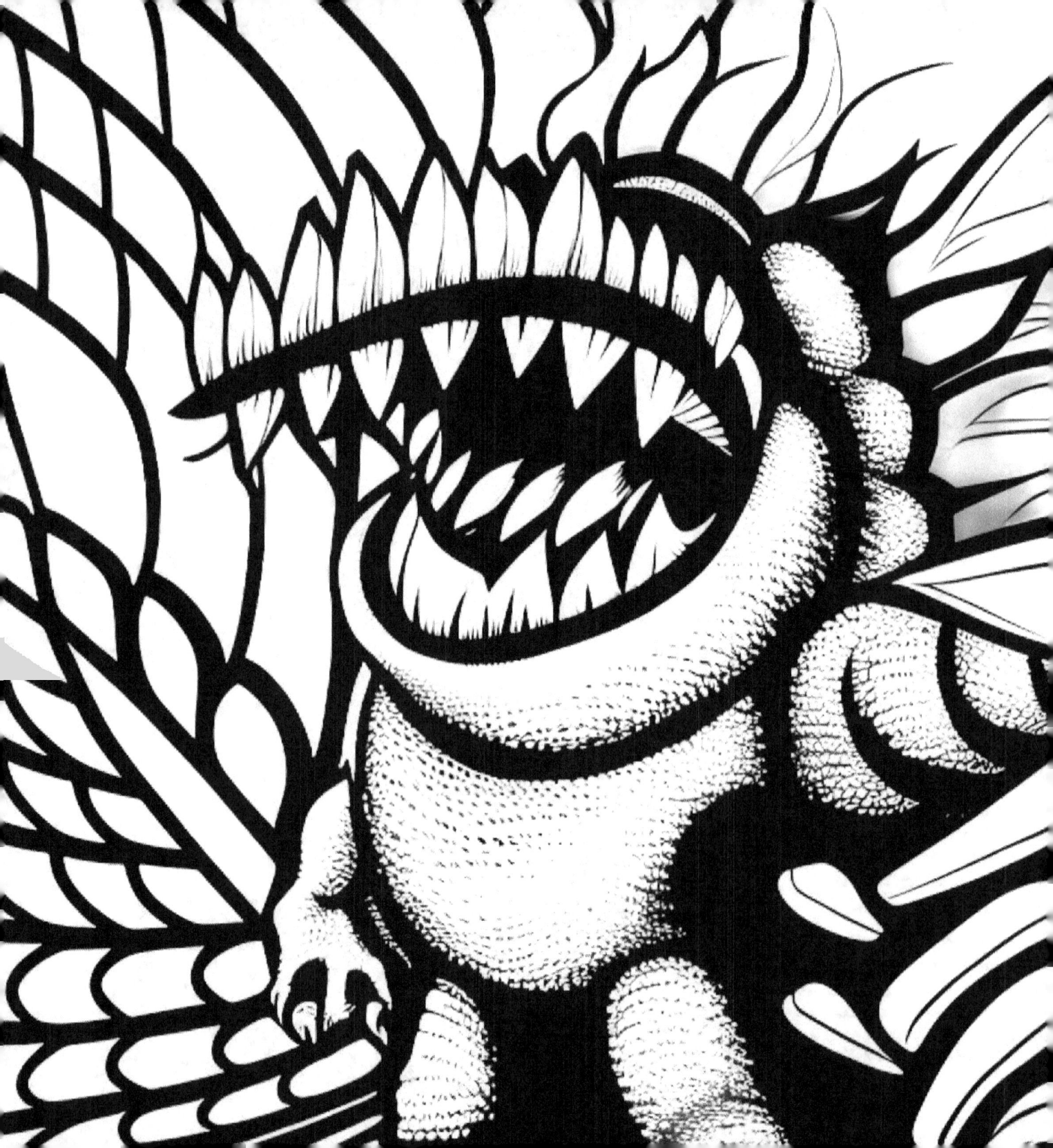

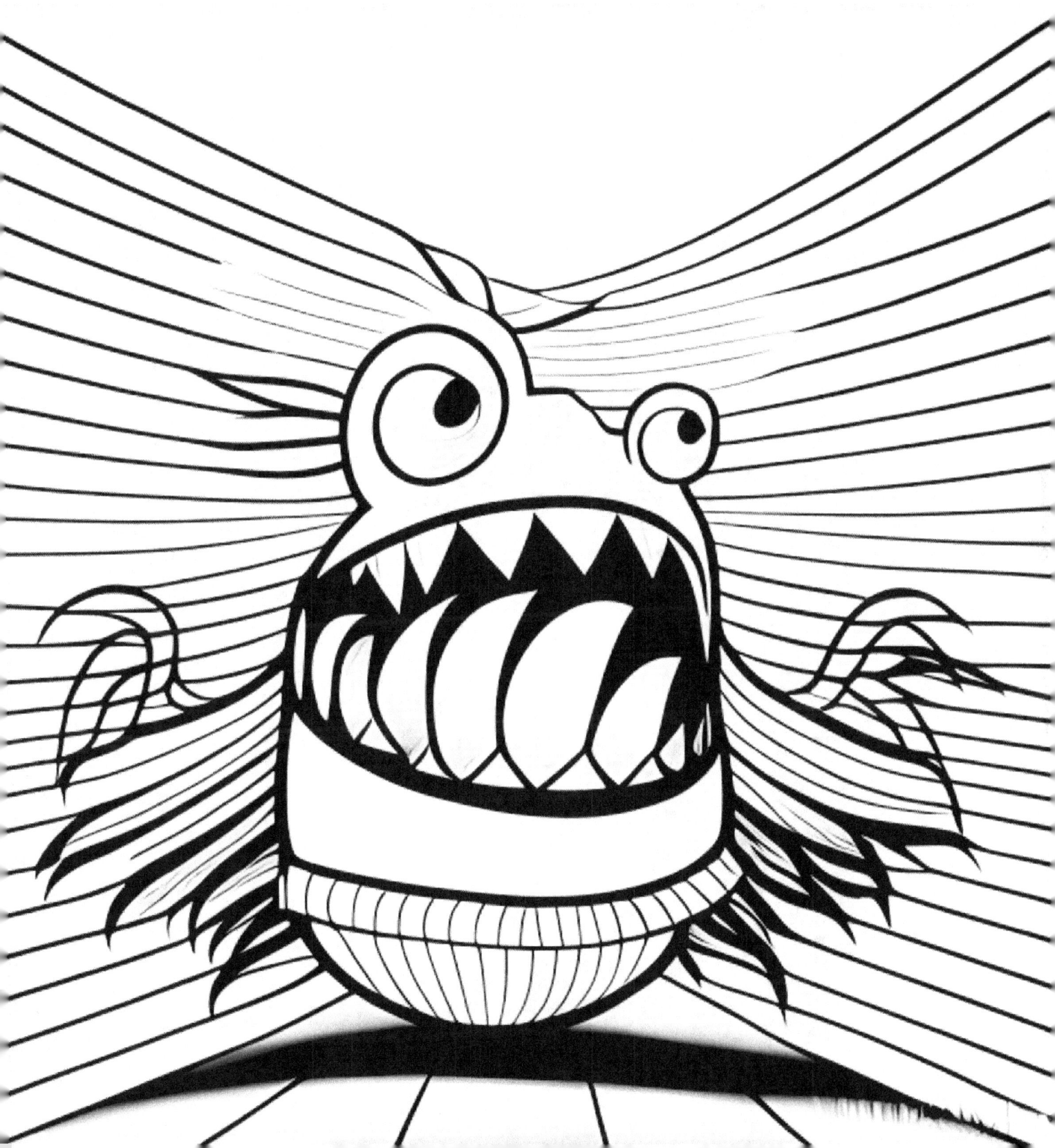

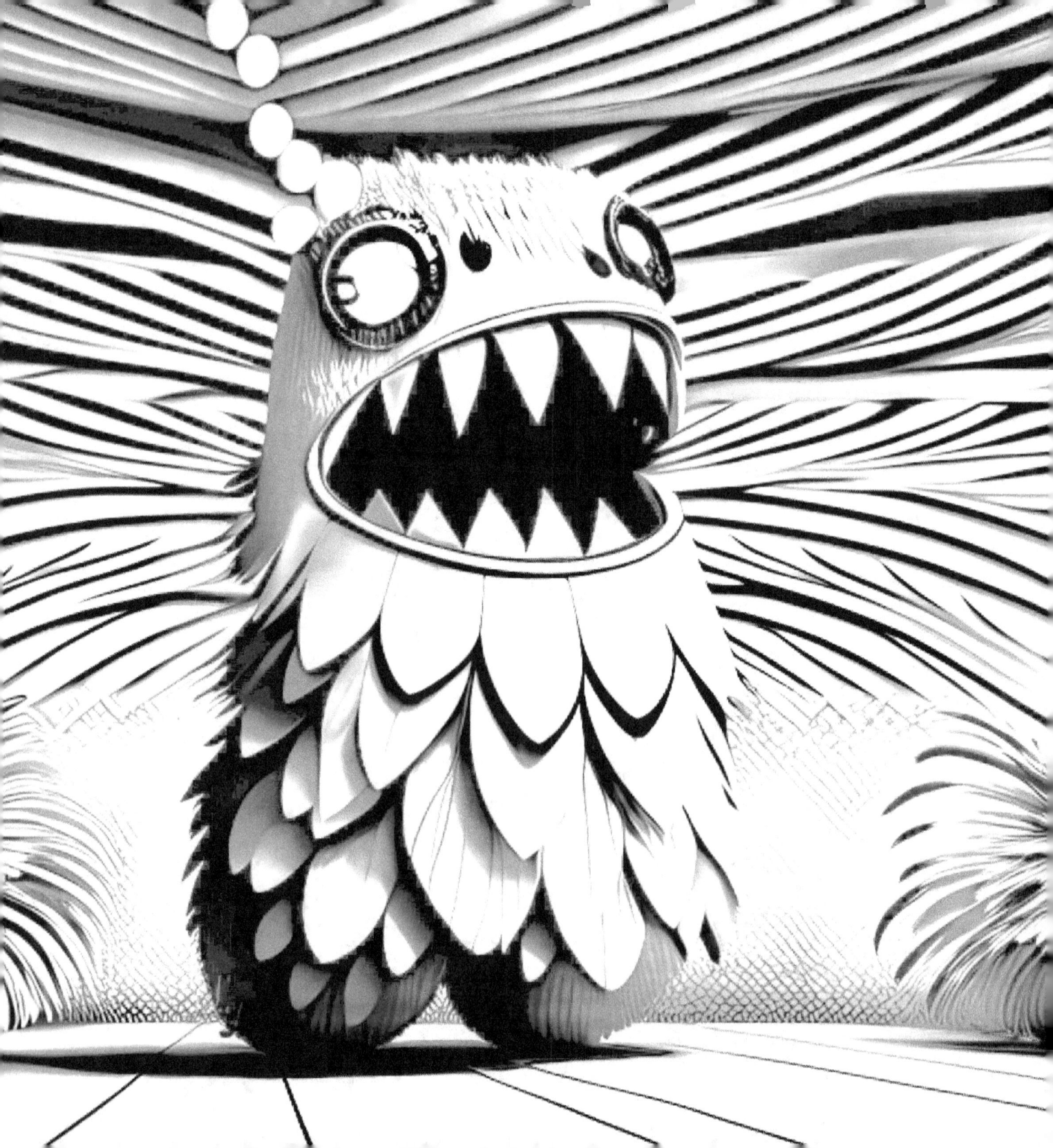

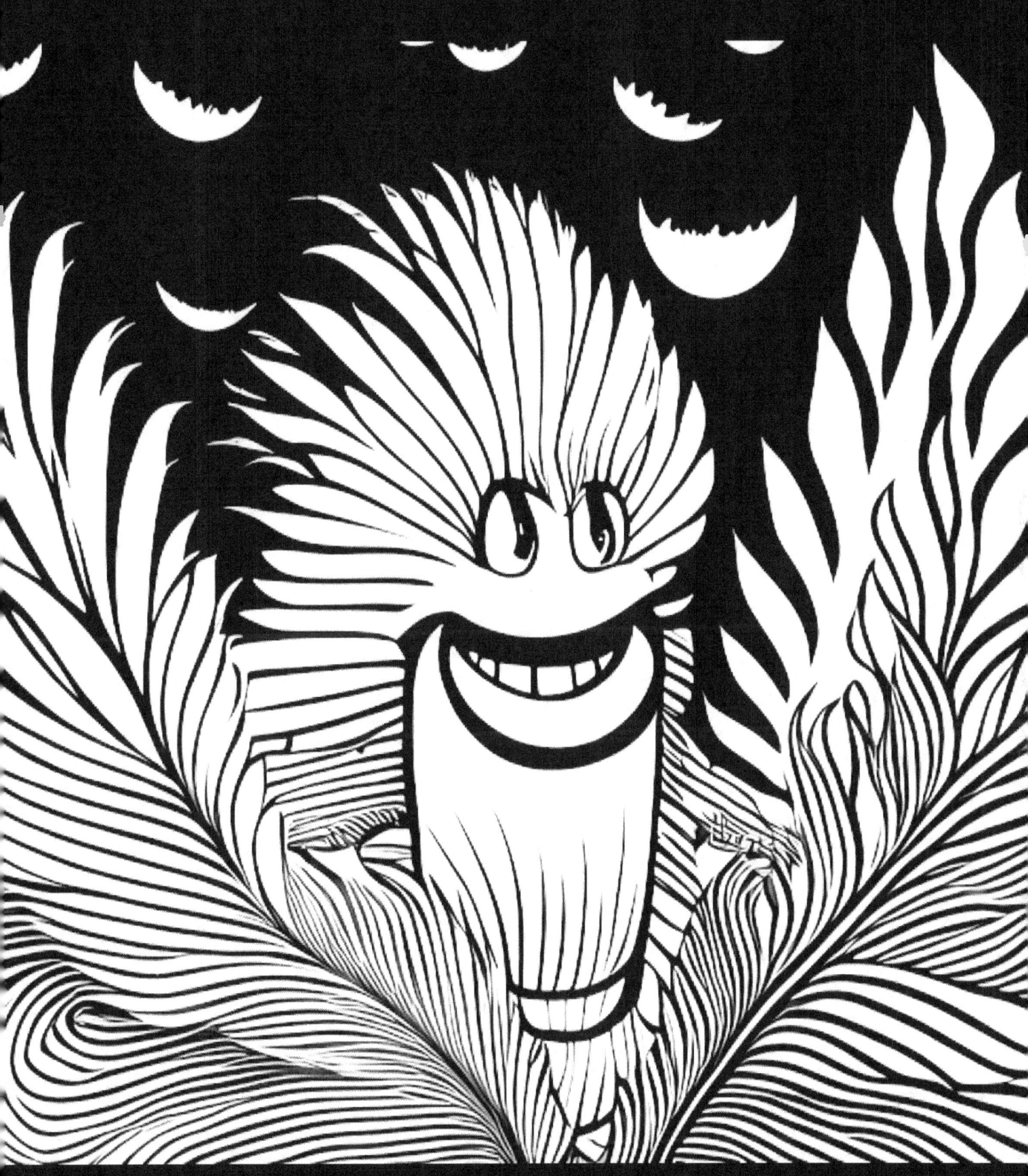

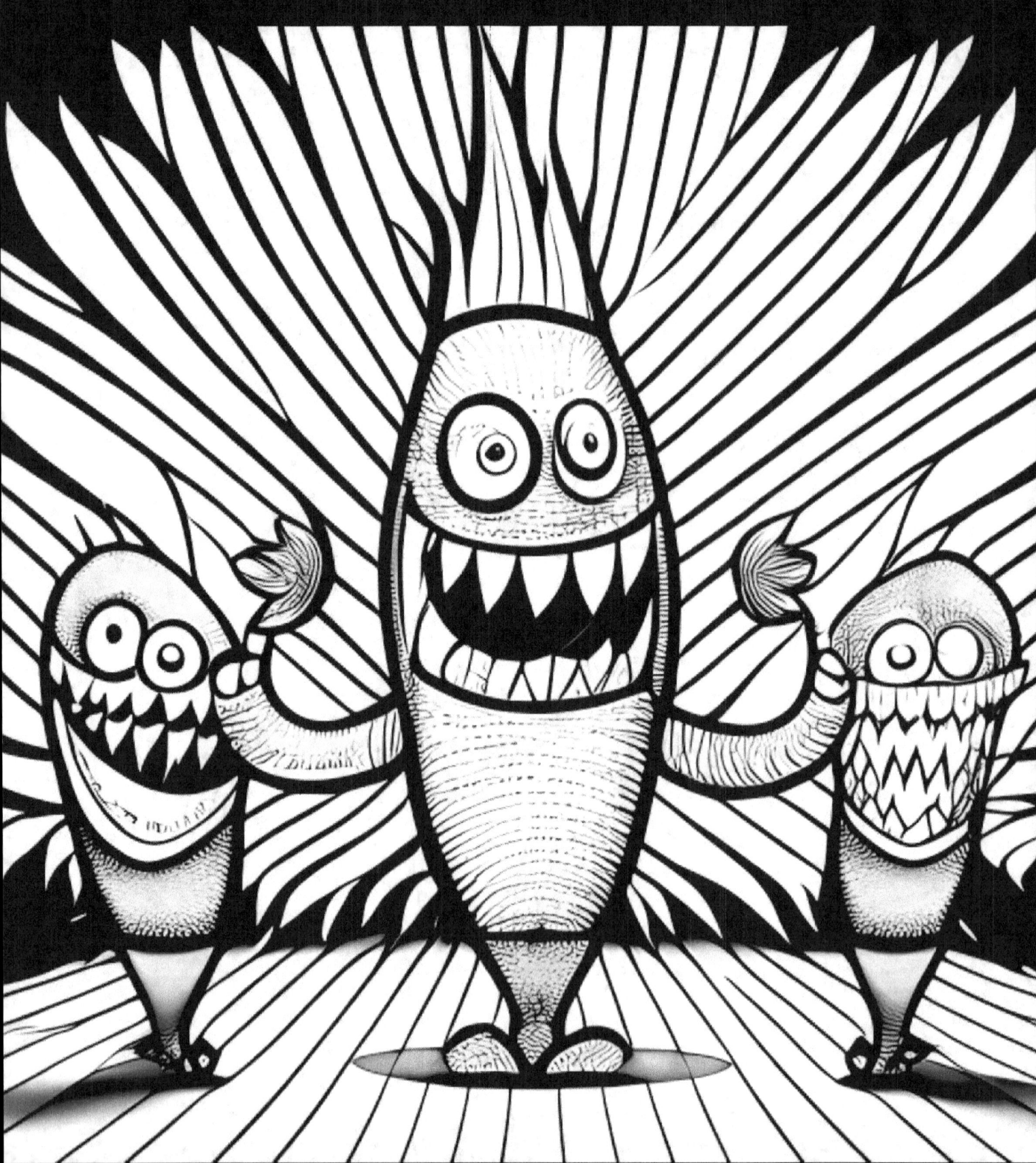

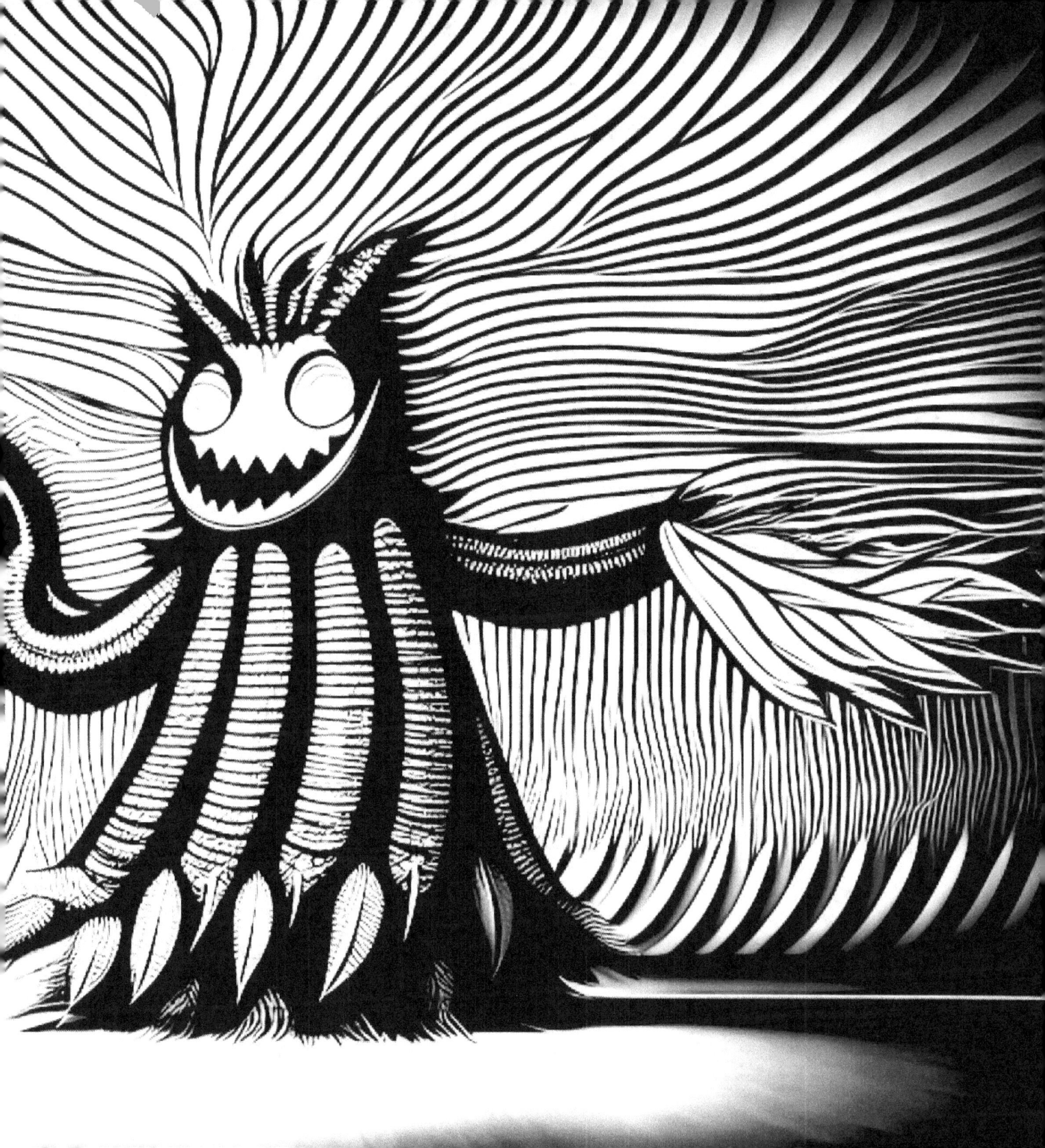

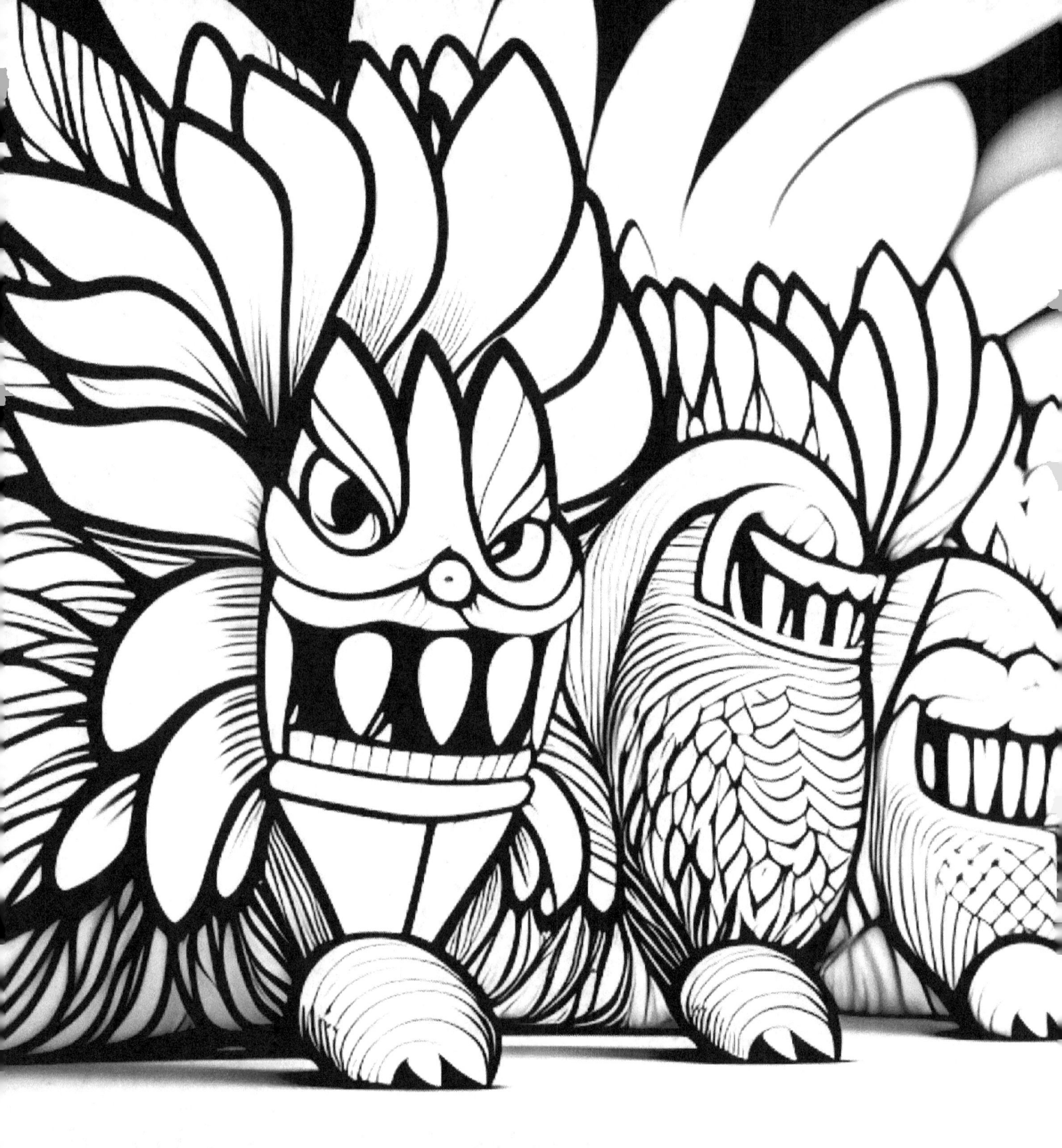

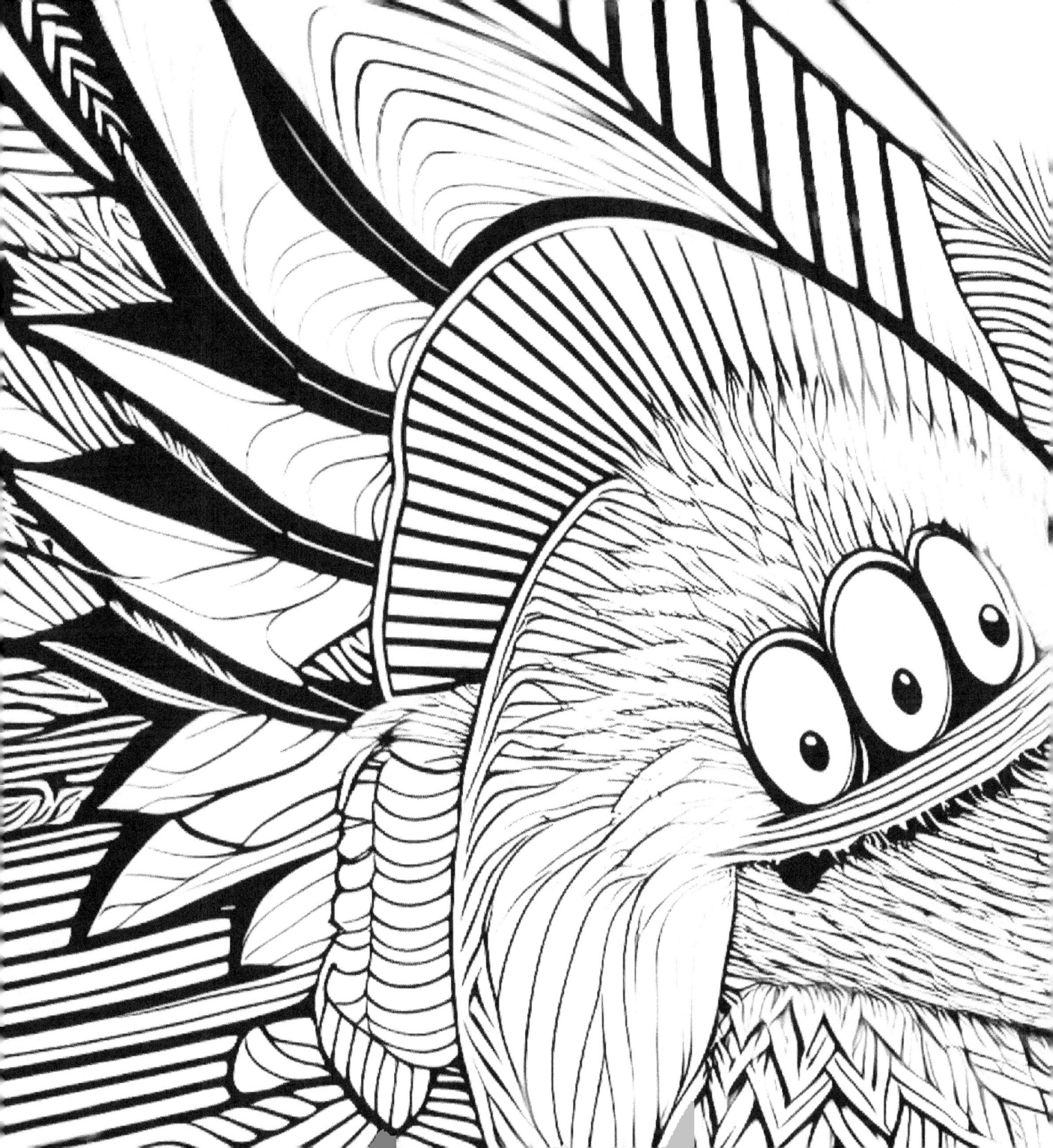

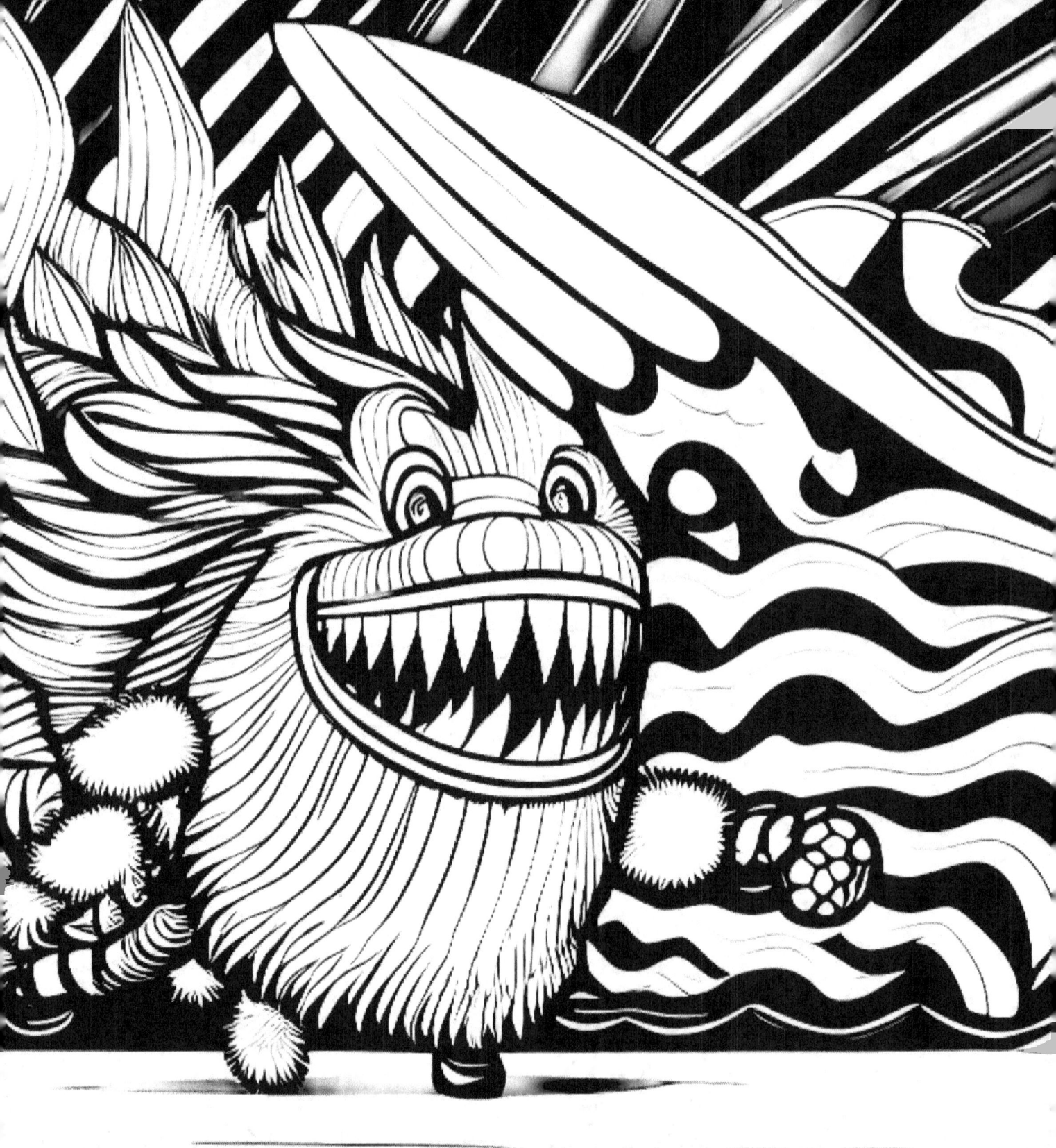

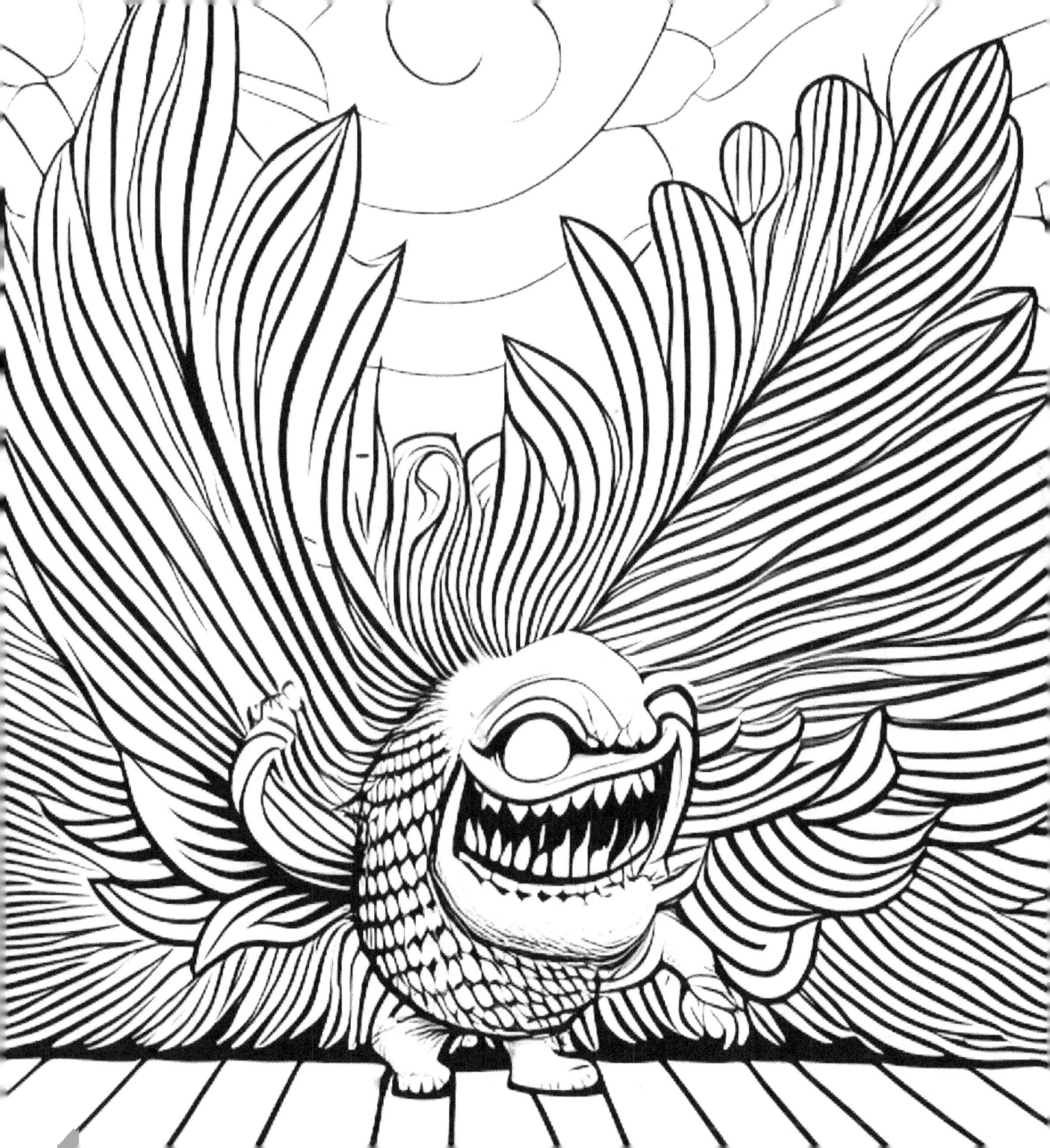

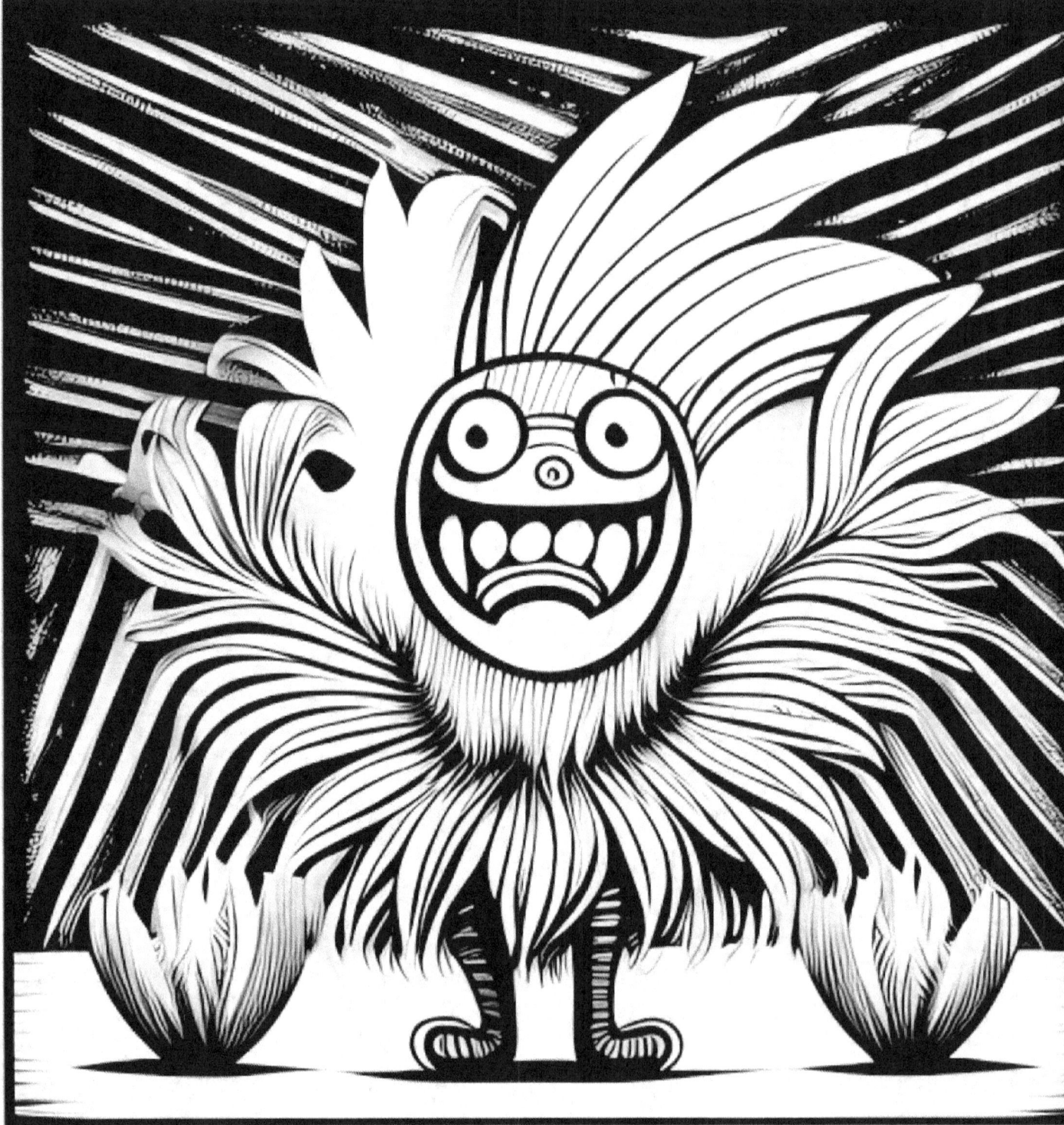

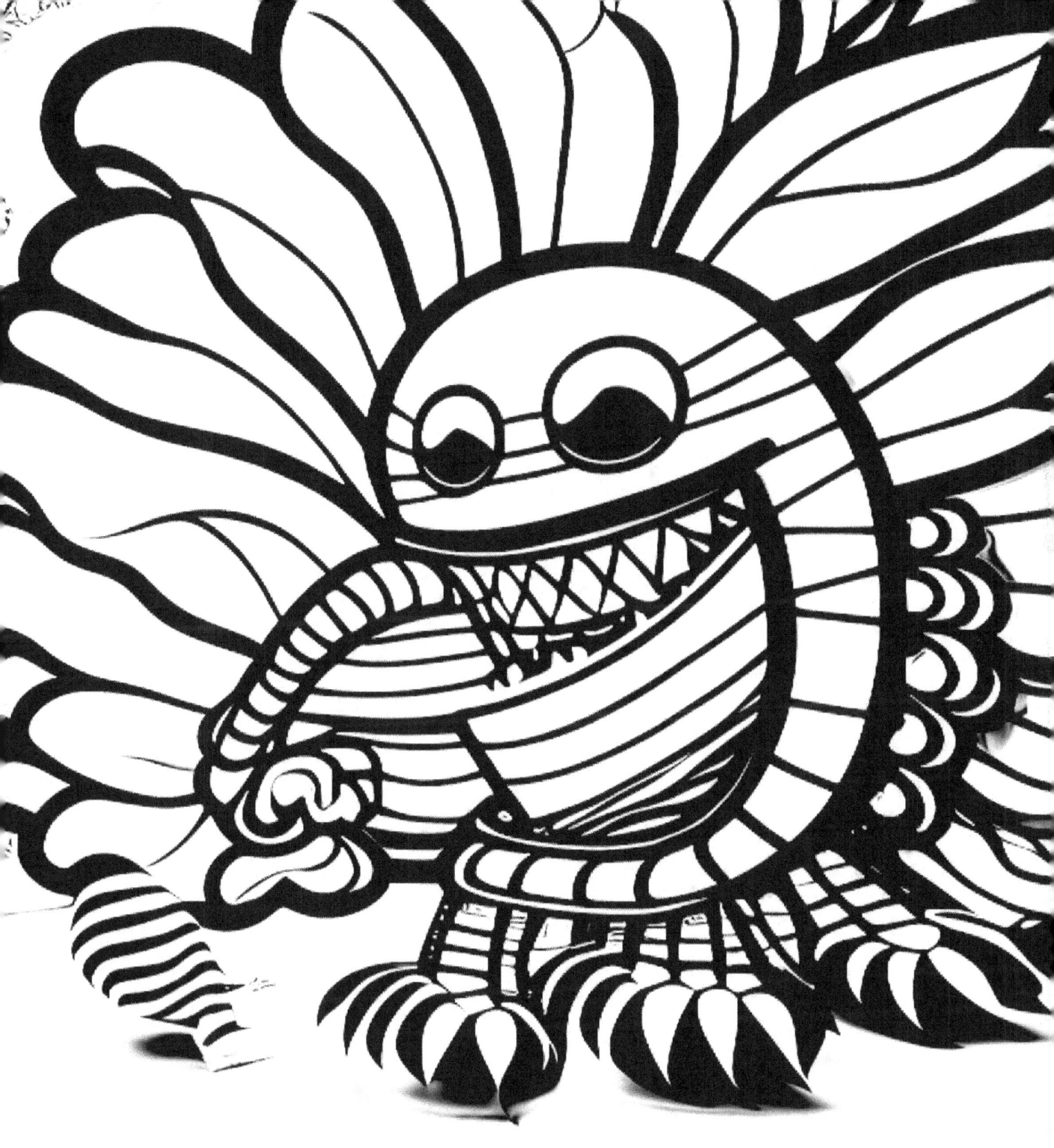

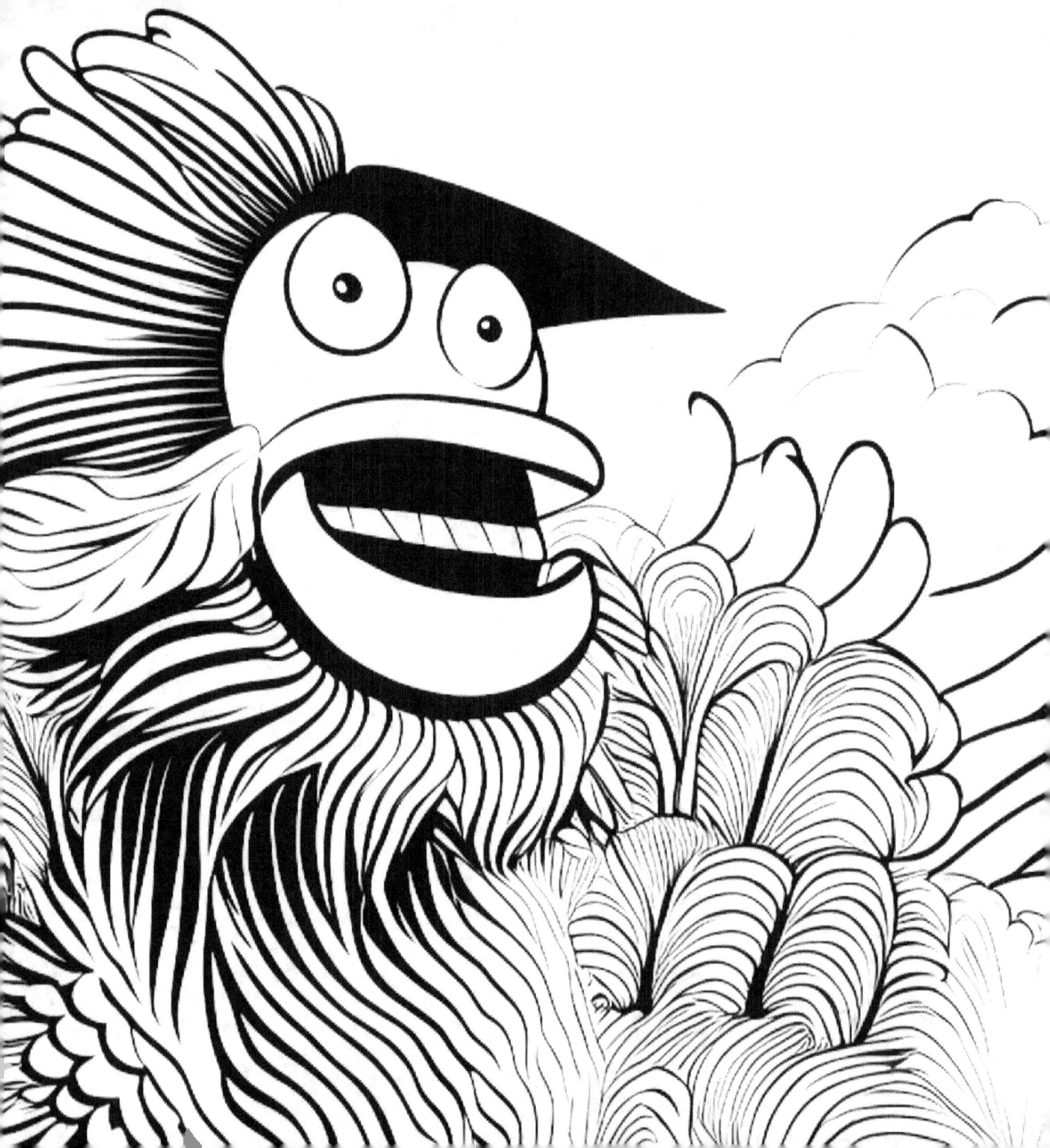

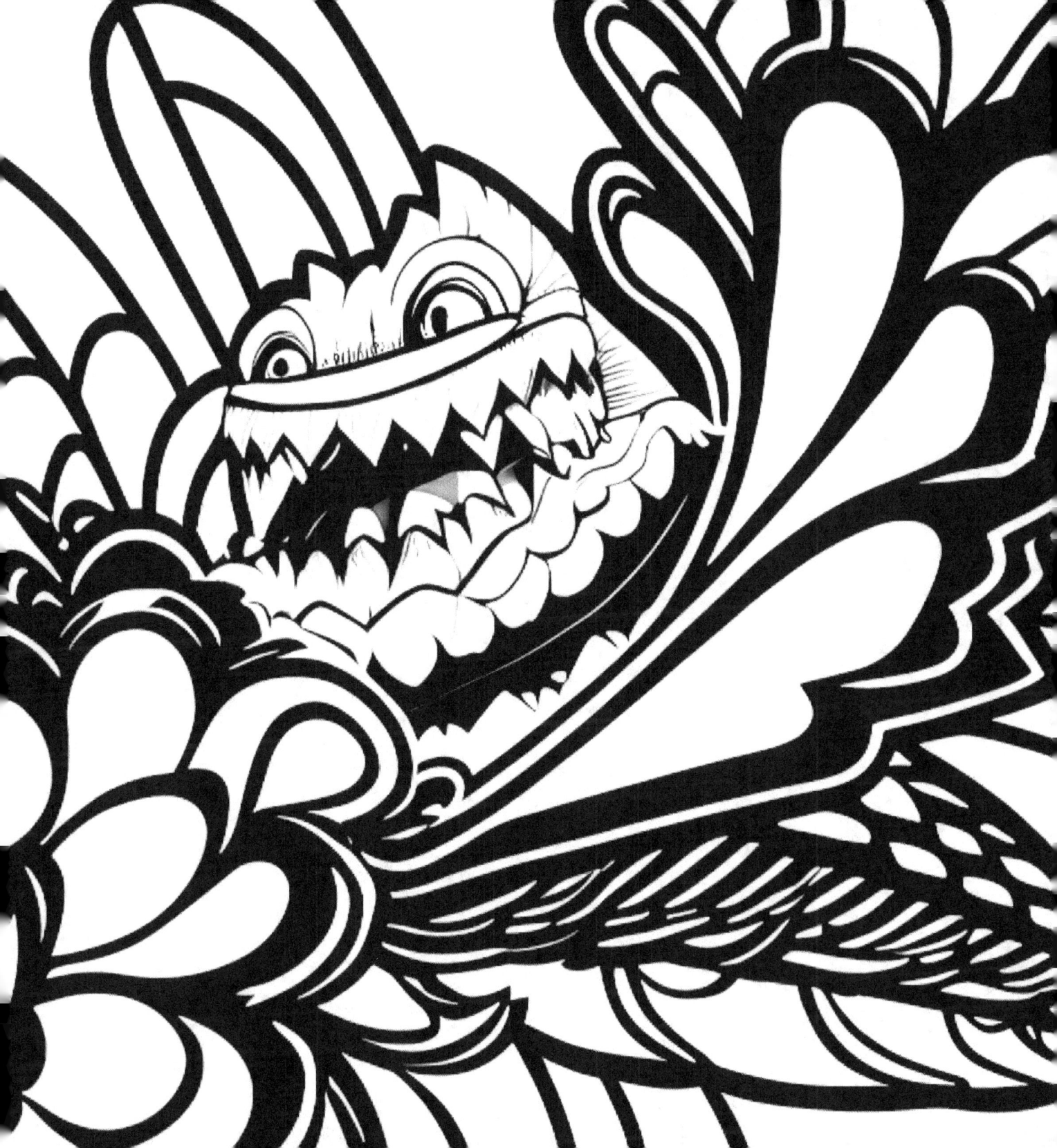

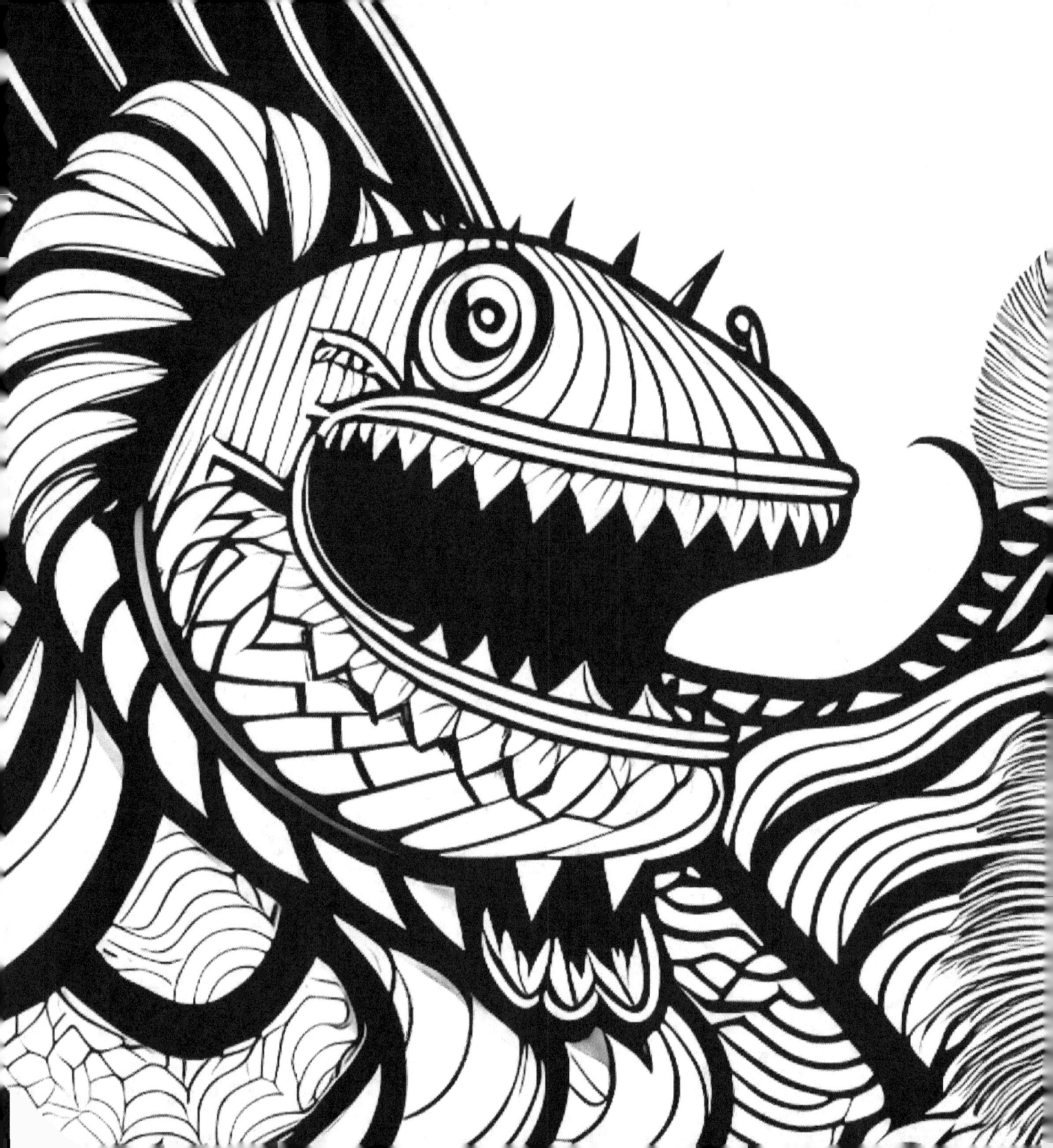

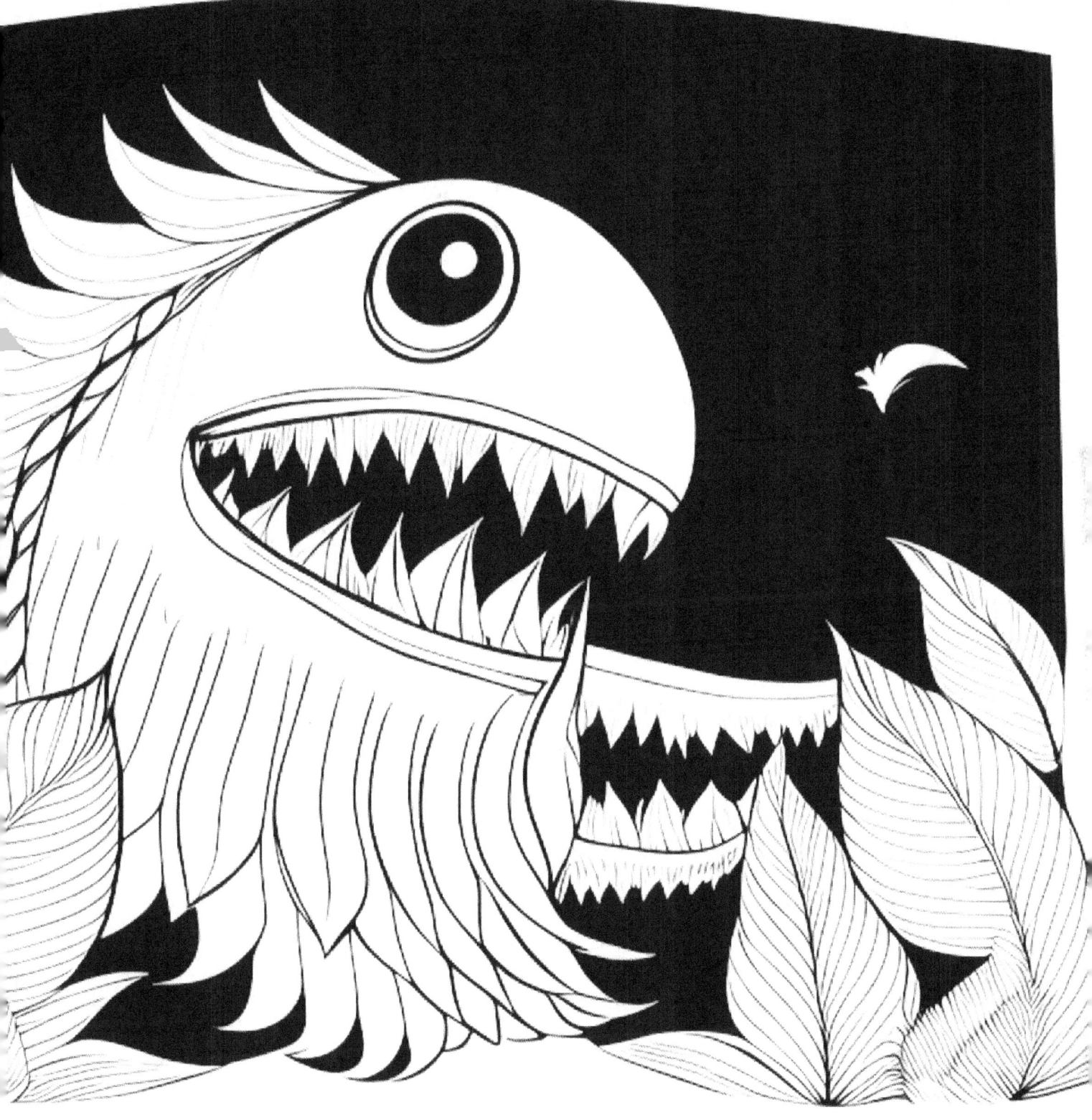

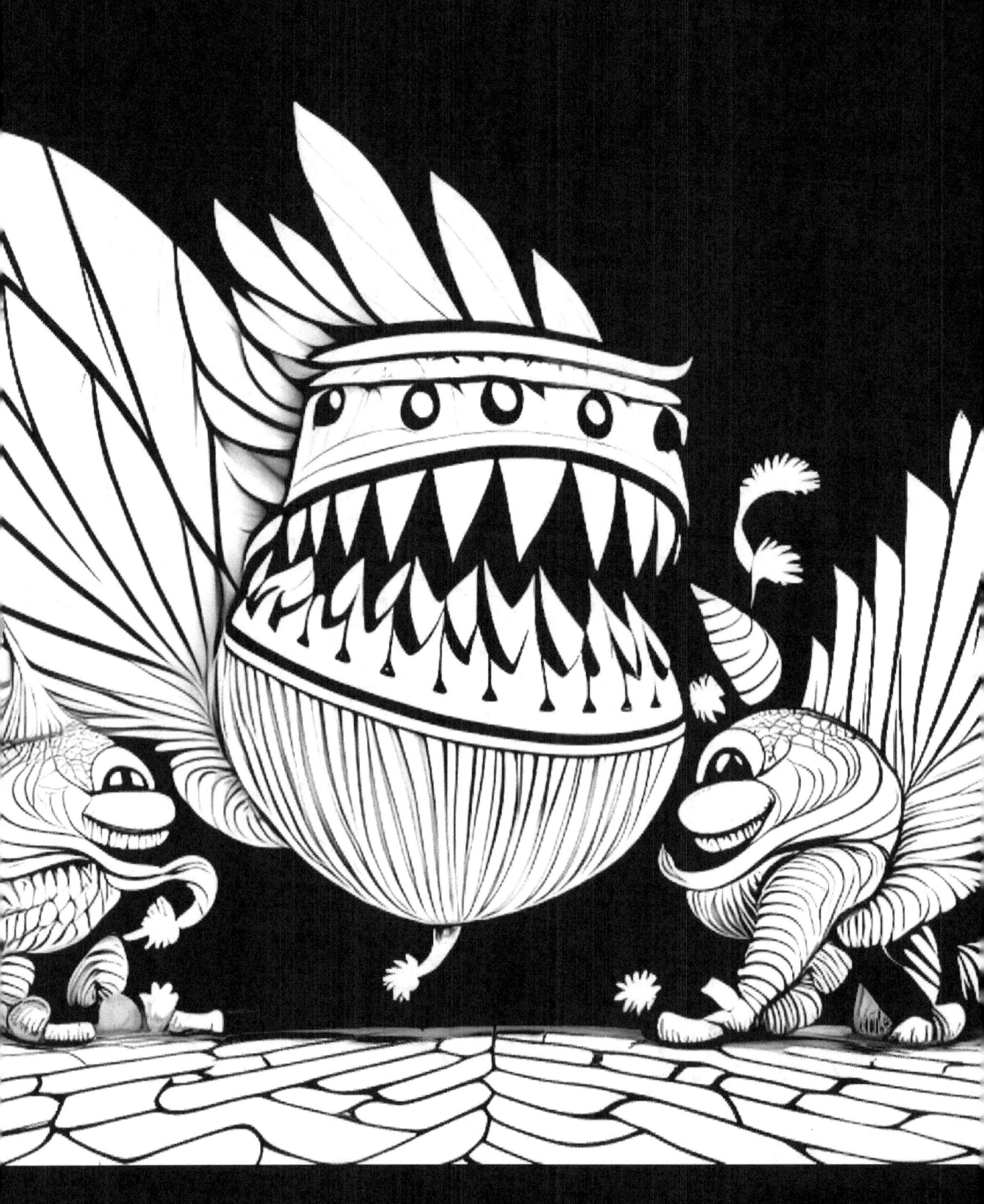

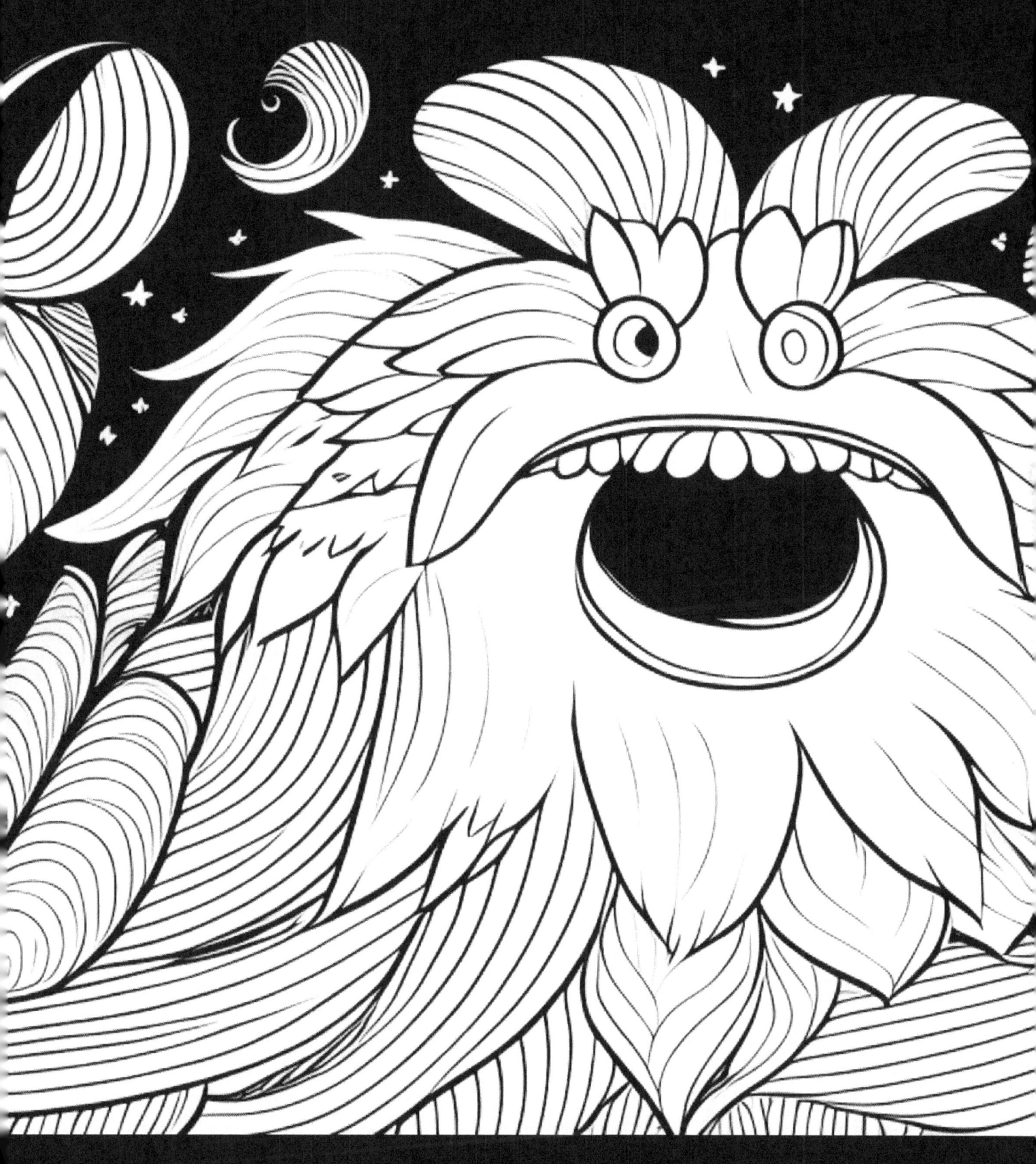